You Will See Hoopoes

DATE DUE

Demco

You Will See Hoopoes
Expanding your Vision of God

Lenna Lidstone

Illustrations by Gunnel Engqvist

OM publishing

First Published 2000 by OM Publishing
Reprinted 2001

07 06 05 04 03 02 01   8 7 6 5 4 3 2

OM Publishing is an imprint of Paternoster Publishing,
PO Box 300, Carlisle, Cumbria, CA3 0QS, UK
and Paternoster Publishing USA
Box 1047, Waynesboro, GA 30830-2047
www.paternoster-publishing.com

British Library Cataloguing in Publication Data

A catalogue record for this book is available
from the British Library
1-85078-370-5

Typeset by WestKey Ltd., Falmouth, Cornwall
Cover design by Diane Bainbridge
Printed in Great Britain by
Omnia Books Limited, Glasgow

Dedicated to Ayshe,
through whose friendship
I learned so much,

and in memory of
Elsie Alexander,
who encouraged me to go
in search of hoopoes.

Contents

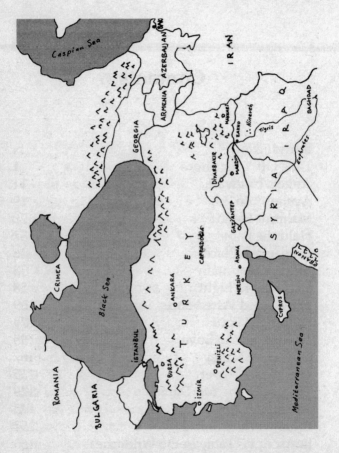

Turkey

Introduction

May 1980

I felt so heavy on the inside – as if I'd swallowed a mountain. Maybe I had! Perhaps in my commitment to God I'd bitten off more than I could chew. The ache inside made it impossible to give myself to the conversations going on around me.

My husband, Julyan, and I had driven down from Manchester early in the morning for this special day of prayer for Turkey. It was important to us, for in just a few months we would be in Ankara, Turkey's capital city, beginning our work with Operation Mobilisation. It was a lovely sunny day in London and our hosts, Ichthus Fellowship, had just served us take-away Turkish kebabs for lunch in the church garden. What a great opportunity to mingle and get to know folk with a similar vision and burden to ourselves – folk who cared and prayed about this large unevangelised country. Why, then, did I feel so weighed down?

The awful ache had crept in as I'd listened to some testimonies in the morning session. People who had worked in Turkey or been in close contact with the work there had talked about some of their experiences. It all seemed very serious, emotionally quite depressing, not like the happy summer missions and camps I'd been involved in. Physically, I cringed as a lady related in some detail the trauma of giving birth in a Turkish hospital. Spiritually, it seemed so unrewarding as they talked about years of work with little to show for it. There had been many tears yet little fruit. Could I really follow in their footsteps? Did I have the necessary strength of character, the stickability required for the long haul? I didn't feel cut out for the job. Even more painful, I sensed that as the realities of the situation came closer, I didn't even want to be cut out for the job!

It was different at Bible School in Glasgow where Julyan and I met. We were both involved in the Middle East prayer group and these times of prayer were the highlight of my week. Some of the others in the group were also heading for Muslim countries, one couple to Pakistan and another to Senegal. As we prayed we had joy and expectancy that we were on the threshold of God's new move in the Islamic world. And yet, even then, if I were honest, it wasn't all triumphalistic fervour. We'd had our sombre moments. Just weeks before our wedding news had come of the murder of Dave Goodman, a Christian worker in Adana. He had been shot on his doorstep, leaving his wife pregnant with their first baby.

This had been especially poignant for us, as Dave had written to Julyan while he was praying about his future and our relationship. His letter had really helped Julyan decide to go to Turkey. Now Dave was dead. I remembered the anguish I had felt then, as I considered the sacrifice that our call to that land could mean. Now the ache was back again. Could God be calling us to a work that would be slow and costly? Yet it was too late to change my mind. My commitment had been made. God had already brought me to that point.

In the middle of my Bible College course I had gone to Belgium for short-term summer work. Before going out in our teams, we had a week's conference at a university campus. That week was quite stressful for me as I had such a bad cold. The burning in my throat made singing practically impossible, and I found it hard to keep my nose in tissues for a whole meeting. All the girls in my dormitory knew about it. They had to suffer my snoring at night! One morning I found a note on my pillow.

It said 'Praise God for your cold, there's a blessing in it!'

That evening I came late to the auditorium and sat alone at the back. The rows of seats were tiered which meant I was quite far from the platform. With a world map and pointer, the speaker began to take us through the world situation. Not one to be moved by statistics, I was surprised by my reaction to the figures.

'20% of the world is Muslim yet only 2–3% of the church's missionary force is focused amongst them.'

Islam, the Muslim world, the scarcity of workers were challenging my heart. I'd been praying for the Middle East for some time and even though I had one more year at Bible School the question of 'What next?' was on my mind.

George Verwer followed, with a challenge to fresh commitment to the Lord. Was God speaking to anyone about a specific area that needed to be given to him? If so, we should stand. I remember the argument I had with myself. Yes, I'd felt challenged. Yes, my heart was drawn to the Middle East, but I did have one more year at college. There was no hurry. Also, I did have this dreadful cold. Surely God wouldn't want me to make such a big decision when I felt so weak and pathetic...

Suddenly, as I looked down at the map from the back row of the auditorium I began to see the truth of Ephesians 2:6. God had 'raised me up and seated me in the heavenly realm'. The world looked small! Faith surged through me and I stood up.

'If you'll take me I'll go,' I prayed.

By faith, I could see the situation from God's perspective. It didn't matter that I was weak and pathetic. With Christ the challenge of the Muslim world was not too big. World evangelisation, good news for the poor, building his church – nothing was impossible with Christ! And as I stood up, quite freely, knowing that God would still love me even if I stayed in my seat, God's favour seemed to settle on my head, his pleasure touching me like the 'Well done' pat of his hand and my cold was gone. There had been a blessing in it after all!

No, I couldn't doubt God or his will. In our final year at college he had graciously put Julyan and myself together and confirmed again and again that our place in the Middle East was Turkey. Yet Julyan seemed so much better prepared. His father was an engineer, working in many parts of the world. Travel and living abroad were in his family's blood. But what about me? I had never even been inside an aeroplane.

Julyan's church had asked us to spend this first year of marriage with them before being sent out. Even Manchester had given me a dose of culture shock with folks' insistence on putting the milk in the tea cups first – very difficult for a Scot who drinks her tea black! How would I cope with the cultural challenges of a country so vastly different from Scotland? Julyan had worked in India prior to Bible college. He had travelled through Turkey several times and had even done a period of short-term work there. Would I hold him back? These feelings of inadequacy were there again and I didn't know if I could make it.

I felt an arm come around my shoulder. It was the mother of yet another Christian worker from Turkey. No doubt she had been watching me and had guessed how I was feeling. Coming alongside, she wanted in some way to encourage me.

'Don't worry about going to Turkey,' she said. 'It's really a wonderful place,' and then, with apparent sudden inspiration, she added, 'Just think, my dear, you will see hoopoes!'

I smiled and thanked her. My heart had warmed to the words and I kept repeating them to myself.

'You will see hoopoes! You will see hoopoes!'

It seemed such an odd thing to say in order to encourage a would-be missionary. Most of my friends wouldn't even know what a hoopoe was. Yet I did know. I loved bird-watching and my mother-in-law had bought me the relevant bird book for Turkey. Already, I had worked out that though many birds would be the same as those seen in Britain, there would be some beautiful exceptions. I would see blue roller birds lining the country roads, swinging from the telephone wires. Perhaps I might glimpse a golden oriole in the woods, shy, yet quite distinctive in black and yellow. Travelling across some farmland I might meet a hoopoe, unmistakable with its pinkish cinnamon plumage, black and white striped wings and prominent black-tipped crest.

Yes, I knew what a hoopoe was. These words of encouragement were surely just for me. I was blessed to be reminded of how personal our God is but as I meditated on the words some more, I found God was talking to me about more than just birds. He would show me aspects of his beauty in Turkey that he wouldn't be able to show me if I stayed in Britain. Many lessons would be similar but some would be quite special to my going. No, if I wanted to see spiritual hoopoes, if I wanted God to show me special acts of his grace, special wonders of his love, I had no choice but to fly with him.

1

Take Off Your Shoes

The pastor read the benediction from Jude: 'Now unto him who is able to keep you from falling…'. A noisy jet aeroplane zoomed overhead and God did what an expert in aerodynamics had failed to do earlier in the week. He gave me peace about the flight. I felt God was taking my fear of heights seriously and had met me just in time.

We flew the next day, arriving in Ankara during the hottest week of the summer. My senses were all heightened. I quickly took in the unfamiliar sounds of mosques and street sellers, the smells of drains and spices, the potholed pavements, mangy cats and apparent absence of the colour green in this concrete jungle of apartment blocks. The main aim of this week's 'holiday' was the signing of a lease on our flat, to enable those families leaving Turkey to store the furniture and household items that they would be passing on to us.

Most of the foreign workers we met that week were on their way out, for one reason or another. A professor, after working in Ankara for ten years, had not had his work permit renewed to lecture at the university. Two families were leaving because of ill health. Other problems we encountered included the young son of a couple staying, who had had diarrhoea for many months. Another was bothered by sickness and the pressure of a demanding job. The atmosphere was heavy. We didn't meet any Turkish believers. There were very few, anyway, and they had all left the city for the summer.

Politically, the country was unstable. There were frequent clashes between secular leftists and fundamental right-wing extremists and in the evenings we could hear occasional gunfire. Stomach trouble hit me on the second day, leaving me nauseous for the rest of the week. We had been challenged on the flight by the verse in Isaiah 61:3 to put on a garment of praise but instead I was crying myself to sleep at night.

Our flat had been found for us. It was in the kind of neighbourhood that was respectable without being upper-class, an unusual choice for foreigners but not impossible. The flat was on the second floor, clean and bright with a balcony at the front. The kitchen was small but adequate, and the toilet was squat style. I later realised that this was preferable in times of water shortage as there is no U-bend. We liked it and we enjoyed our visit to our new landlord. As we entered his home we took off our shoes, a custom common throughout the Middle East. Little did I realise that this simple gesture would become to me a beautiful hoopoe, helping me through the early years of adjusting. The signing of the house contract was accompanied by numerous glasses of tea. It was very sweet but at least there was no milk in it! Maybe there was hope for me after all.

On returning to Manchester, I was regaling a friend with my experience and was overheard by a missionary who had just returned from Ethiopia. I was telling of a visit to a park that was hardly recognisable as there were spaces between the blades of grass! Although I'd often complained about the British weather I'd completely taken for granted the greenness that it produced.

'Oh, but you mustn't compare!' she interrupted.

Her mild rebuke went deep. This was probably the most basic of basics of overseas Christian service.

In October 1980, we set out again for Turkey, this time travelling overland by car, with two girls, one American and one German, who would be part of our team. The long trip helped us to get to know each other and also enabled me to adjust to the changes that were all more gradual. When we arrived in Ankara this time, I was amazed to see tree-lined streets, grassy patches here and there, and little children's play areas in amongst the concrete. I seemed to be looking through new eyes.

Entering Turkey, we were surprised by the sight that met us. Everywhere we looked it seemed that sheep were being slaughtered. What was going on? Was this the normal every-day meat markets or something more? Then we noticed many family groups in their best clothes carrying flowers and obviously on their way to visit relatives. Slowly it dawned on us that it was the first day of *Kurban Bayrami*, the biggest religious holiday in the Muslim world when they sacrifice sheep to remember God's provision of a ram in the place of Abraham's son. How we longed to tell them about Jesus, the Lamb of God who takes away the sin of the world.

This would not be as easy as it seemed, and one of my hardest struggles was with the language. Not only would I have to learn to talk Turkish but also to think Turkish which seemed backwards. We had classes that filled us with grammar. We had tapes of drills and books which required more discipline and dedication than I could muster, and language helpers who didn't know how to help. Julyan, with his linguistic ability and joy of study, was making such progress that when the little fellowship began meeting in our home after only one year, he was praying and preaching quite adequately.

It was so hard for me to speak without understanding everything in detail. One teacher we had used to drum his fingers on the desk as he waited for my answer. Then he would throw his head backwards while making a loud tutting sound. Culturally the body language simply meant 'No', but the impression of disgust I received did little for my self-confidence. The emotional ups and downs of early pregnancy in that first year didn't help, but even by the end of our second year, my progress was poor. Language-learning for me became such a burden that I knew it was quenching the Spirit within me. When I analysed the burden it was full of accusations, such as:

'If you really loved God you would study harder.'

'If you really loved the people you would learn their language.'

Had I been single, I would probably have gone home at this point feeling I'd got my calling wrong. The sense of failure was almost too hard to bear.

Fortunately, we attended a conference with a delightful couple called Tom and Elizabeth Brewster. He had pioneered a new language-learning approach called 'Lamp' or 'Language Acquisition Made Practical.' As he spoke I sensed a feeling of hope kindled within me and I hung onto his catchphrase:

'Language-learning is Relationship is Ministry.'

It seemed so obvious. Relationship was surely the key. I began to understand my problem. All my life I'd loved talking. I'd never been a good listener and yet it was so vital to any friendship. It was also the key to learning a foreign language. In a nutshell, bad listeners make bad language-learners! Here was my chance to allow God to develop all my senses and help me build better friendships.

Somehow I had felt that when I learned Turkish I could begin to 'minister', really serve God, and yet I knew it would be like climbing a mountain and finding there was yet another peak. It was so liberating to think that 'ministry' was the life of Christ touching others through me. I determined to allow God to love the Turkish people through me by smile, by wave, by touch, by embrace and any words I could manage. Of course, I would never fully make it, get it, know it when it came to language and culture. I was a learner and I always would be. My new role began to excite me. In every relationship I would be at the listening, learning, lowly end. Perhaps it was there that people would find Jesus.

Our landlord sold our house and we had to move with Emma, our little girl, who was almost two years old. The new flat was in a different area of town where the neighbours were aggressively friendly. We had ladies' afternoons that rotated round the homes in the building. Emma with a ball of wool and a crochet hook would pretend to do her handicraft with the rest of us. It was just what I needed and my fluency improved. The people in the building opposite were friendly too, and they would sit around on the flat roof in a more 'villagey' manner with the Turkish tea and cake served informally. If they saw me on my balcony they would beckon me to come over. One lady played a drum called a *darbuka* and others would sing and sometimes dance. Often they would talk about God and ask me about my faith. In my efforts to explain what I believed I would tell stories from the gospels.

During one such visit a neighbour was very distressed about a number of family problems. I wanted to tell the story of Jesus calming the storm. This was tricky as I couldn't remember the words for boat, sea or storm! It became a game of charades as I acted it out. My Turkish friends were so patient but, oh, the joy and relief when someone guessed right and the story continued. At last the point was made. We sat still and quiet for a few moments as God seemed to come down with his peace. Inwardly I still groaned over my level of language but I also marvelled that God could do so much with so little. He cared enough to bless us all despite my feeble efforts and surely these ladies wouldn't forget a story they had helped to tell.

My new attitude helped me in many ways. So often I'd been frustrated when friends failed to recognise my attempts at Turkish cooking. I always cut my onion too big or added too little oil. My spices would be wrong or lacking. Once during a visit I was asked what I had cooked.

'Oh, Scottish *dolma*,' (stuffed peppers) I replied.

As we were eating they were curious.

'Do you eat *dolma* in Scotland?'

'Not really, but as my hands are Scottish, my *dolma* will always be Scottish, too.'

The effect was amazing.

'They are just like the *dolma* my Grandma used to make!' they exclaimed.

What praise!

In the early years God was teaching me about the humble path of being a learner. Surely I'd come to tell and to teach but there was so much to learn along the way. Now when I visited a friend and removed my shoes at the door, I could feel the humility of the gesture. It wasn't just to keep my host's carpet clean but to say, 'This is your domain and I'm treading lightly. I've left the symbol of my own authority outside.' Only the police march into a home with their shoes on! And as the host clothed my feet in slippers like her own, I would understand:

'My home is your home. Welcome.'

Many times in these first years in Turkey, pride would have rendered me useless, but God was faithful and proved 'able to keep me from falling'. I began to feel more and more at home. Perhaps in my heart I'd taken off my shoes. Perhaps like Moses before the burning bush, this attitude was the path to divine authority for mission.

2

Angels Unaware

In the New Testament the writer to the Hebrews urges us to be hospitable. Hebrews 13:2 states, 'Do not forget to entertain strangers, for by so doing some people have entertained angels without knowing it.' I wondered how many visitors I would have to receive before I got an angel? Fifty? A hundred? A thousand?

You see, in the Middle East you honour or befriend someone not by inviting them to your home but rather by visiting them in theirs. Hospitality is, therefore, of great importance as it is the appropriate response to being thus honoured. As we were foreigners and new to our apartment block and neighbourhood we had many callers! A Turkish visit followed a pattern and after a while I learned to do it quite well.

First, I would welcome my guests, kissing the ladies on both cheeks and shaking hands with the men if appropriate. If the men were strict

Muslims I would not even look at their faces as that would be offensive, and all my interaction would be with the women. In many Muslim societies men and women go into separate rooms when visiting, but in the cities of Turkey we were able to entertain couples together. Ushering them right in to the most comfortable chairs I would bring slippers for their feet, because they would have removed their shoes at the door. After asking each one in turn how they were and how their families were, I would sprinkle their hands with lemon cologne.

A little more chat and I would slip away to the kitchen and return with a tray of Turkish coffee in small cups. If I had made it well I would manage frothy topping on each one. I would sit near the door and would not drink myself to emphasise how special the visitors were. Each cup would be collected as it was finished so as not to insult a guest by leaving a dirty dish in front of them. Some more chat and I might offer individual bowls of nuts or freshly made popcorn.

It was important not to serve Turkish tea too soon as that would signal the beginning of the end of the visit. There was plenty of time and it had to be drawn out and savoured to the full. There would be no talking at depth, no serious topic or sensitive issue raised until we were drinking tea together, but the earlier part of the visit could not be rushed.

Eventually, I would produce individual plates of savouries and a cake made specially for the visit that could be cut and served in their presence. It was now time to drink tea which I would pour into tiny crystal glasses. A well-known Turkish expression likens the colour of sufficiently brewed tea to that of rabbits' blood – a bright reddish brown. Again I would serve the tea from a tray, putting the sugar lumps in for each guest. I would sit on my chair by the door watching the glasses carefully, ready to pounce with my tray when one was empty. The running back and forward refilling tea glasses could go on for anything up to an hour or more, depending on how much the guests were enjoying their visit. Several times they would refuse more tea but I would manage to persuade them to drink 'just one more glass'.

Our visitors would begin to ask permission to leave amidst Julyan's playful protests:

'But it's so early! The night is yet young!'

This was my signal to slip back to the kitchen and re-emerge with individual plates of fruit to make them stay longer. After the official farewells there was usually a little game of tug-of-war as I tried to help them on with their coats. We would walk together to the road where we would have more goodbyes and waves until they were out of sight.

Although I'd learnt the pattern and could do it like a part in a play, it was sometimes at best just that, a part in a play. At worst, it was a wearisome business. Often I felt I was being forced to go the extra mile and I struggled so much inside with my role. One day, however, I really did catch the spirit of it.

Julyan was teaching English at a language school in town. A neighbour we didn't know too well called in and made an arrangement for an evening that week. Julyan reacted like a Westerner and presumed he had invited us to his home.

The day of the visit had been hectic. I was suffering a lot of nausea with our second baby and we had given lunch to six Iranian refugees who had turned up wanting help filling in forms for visas. This had taken all afternoon. When they left, the house was untidy. All the food was eaten and I felt sick as usual. As it was going to be our first visit to these neighbours I bought some roses, which the florist wrapped beautifully in transparent film and ribbons. I managed to dress nicely and decided the house could wait till the next day.

Suddenly the bell rang and I opened the door. Julyan had misunderstood the arrangement! There on the doorstep were the neighbour and wife from upstairs, their married son and wife, and teenage daughter – five adults and I had nothing to offer – and the living room was a mess.

The family saw the flowers in my hand and a look of sheer delight spread across their faces.

They could hardly believe their good fortune that we had wanted to visit them. Unable to deny themselves such a privilege, they ushered us upstairs with great joy. I was so relieved that my appreciation of their hospitality quite over-whelmed them as I threw my arms around the women who had saved my life! They pulled out all the stops, the married son disappeared home only to return with some cake and the teenage daughter left discreetly to buy nuts from the corner shop. It was a wonderful evening. You would think they had been entertaining angels!

It reminded me of the extravagant response of Zacchaeus when Jesus told him he was coming to his house for tea and the attitude of Jesus to the multitude who visited him in his lonely place. Jesus, the perfect host, refused to send them away but served more than five thousand people with fish and bread. Yes, it was an honour when folk wanted to be with you enough to visit your home and as I asked God to bless my hands and open them more to others I found him energising my serving with his joy.

I had much to learn and many times I wres-tled with selfish, lazy attitudes. Rebekah from the Old Testament became a challenging example for me. In Genesis 24, when asked for a drink by Abraham's servant Eliezer, she quite voluntarily offers to water his ten thirsty camels! This willingness to go the extra mile was the sign chosen to mark Rebekah as a suitable bride for Abraham's son, Isaac. Surely nothing less would make a fitting bride for the Son of God. Before arriving in Turkey I had often prayed, saying:

'I only want to serve you and the Turkish people.'

I hadn't expected God to take my words quite so literally and yet through practical hospitality and the opening of my home, he was teaching me an attitude that should characterise all our service to God. Yes, as a member of Christ's bride, the church, I had to learn again that joy-filled service is the only appropriate response to the tremendous visitation of Christ to my life.

The church in Turkey was tiny, a few small groups meeting in the major cities. At this pioneering stage of development, inevitably foreign workers were doing most of the Bible-teaching and the organising and financing of projects like the New Testament translation and Bible correspondence course. This course was started in the 1960s by OM and is still run from a small office in Istanbul, with the follow-up being done by workers or believers from the nearest city. It was so important that leadership was modelled on and seen as servanthood, and that the spirit of honouring and esteeming one another flowed through everything that was done.

Little had Rebekah realised, as she went about her work, that these ten camels being watered were laden with good gifts for her and her family. Nor had she understood at the time that one of them would carry her all the way to her bridegroom Isaac. In her spontaneous offer of hospitality she had stumbled on a great principle of the Kingdom: it is by giving that we receive. Perhaps I too was stumbling on the truth that I was not expected to live 'extra mile' Christianity in my own strength, but as I was willing to step out and be stretched in my faith, God would work in those around me and I would experience his delight in a cheerful giver.

The three visitors in Genesis 18 really did prove to be 'angels unaware' and, as Abraham served them his best, the Lord reiterated his promise of a son. In true Middle Eastern style we see their relationship established and developed through a home visit and the corresponding giving of hospitality. Water was brought for their feet, bread was baked and a calf prepared and eaten. It must have taken hours and yet the Lord didn't appear to be in a hurry. At last, as they were leaving, walking together, looking out over the land, the business of Sodom was discussed. The Lord said, 'Shall I hide from Abraham what I am about to do?' In the context of trusted friendship God shared his plan and led Abraham into intercession for the city.

As I thought more about 'entertaining angels', I decided to see all my visitors as messengers from God. So often in the years that lay ahead the right person would pass through our home with a timely word or deed to encourage or challenge us. Even more important, I began to hunger for a deeper friendship of trust with the Lord himself, in which he could share his plans with me, walk with me and talk with me about his business as well as mine. I knew the only way would be through many a 'home visit', when I would throw open the doors of my heart in welcome and appreciation of his presence.

3

Ayshe

Ayshe, to whom this book is dedicated, was a frequent visitor and became my best Turkish friend. When we first met she was a student at Ankara university and lived nearby in a flat with another girl. As her English was good, Julyan and I were able to ask questions about subjects way beyond our level of Turkish. We learned about family relationships and village life, education and politics. Of course, we also talked about Islam, Ayshe's own pilgrimage to faith and her struggles to grow as a Christian in the spiritual climate of Turkey in the early 1980s.

Ayshe had been brought up in a village in the south of Turkey. Her parents had gone to be guest workers in Germany when she was seven, leaving her in the care of her grand-mother. There were many superstitions in the village and one common idea that Ayshe found very disturbing was of a bridge, 'as narrow as a hair and as sharp as a sword', that she must cross when she died. Underneath were the flames of hell.

Poor Ayshe would lie awake at night imagining her impossible tightrope walk! Granny explained that if she sacrificed a sheep in this life, perhaps it would carry her across. Ayshe felt doubtful that a dead sheep would have the balance required for such a feat, and she rejected these Muslim notions and with them belief in God altogether. By high school she had moved to live with an uncle in Istanbul. These were sad and lonely years, missing her parents and longing for her father's love and protection.

Each summer her Mum and Dad would visit Turkey bringing gifts for all the family. One year, near the end of their stay, Ayshe rummaged in the suitcase to see if there might be just one more present for her. There at the bottom was a little piece of paper. It was a tract written in Turkish and given by Christians who had befriended her Mum and Dad in Germany. The verse was from the first letter of John 4:16, 'God is Love'. Ayshe had never before thought of 'God' and 'love' in the same sentence.

A while later she met a Swiss girl and her Irish flatmate in Istanbul. They had come to share their faith and despite their newness and limited Turkish were able to introduce Ayshe to Jesus and a God who cared for her. And so

Ayshe found her sheep! At the cross she understood Jesus was her sacrificial lamb. In laying down his life he had become the bridge to the Father of love.

Living in a girls' hostel while attending university in Ankara had not been easy for her. In the politically troubled 1970s, the dormitories were often searched by police. She feared keeping a large cumbersome Turkish Bible there and instead chose a pocket 'Good News' New Testament, and through it taught herself English.

Ayshe helped me to understand the cultural values that seemed so different to the Western way. Relationships were much more important here, with the emphasis on 'being' rather than 'doing'. Once, when I was feeling unwell, Ayshe dropped in to see me.

'Oh dear,' I apologised, 'I can't possibly talk to you today.'

Ayshe looked disappointed and I knew I had hurt her.

'I didn't want you to talk to me. I just wanted to be with you,' she explained.

Had I been her blood sister she would have happily lain down on the bed beside me. And yet I was her sister. We were her family. She had no one closer to her. I began to see the tremendous responsibility we had to Turkish Christians. Ayshe's family were in Germany but others would inevitably 'lose' family and friends as they came to faith in Christ. Would they come into the warmth of Christian community, the extended family of God or would we expect them to be satisfied with a series of meetings instead?

For our Turkish friends, experiencing life together was far more important than following programmes. Westerners who were often highly motivated, goal-orientated individuals with great commitment to 'the work' were considered 'cold'. National believers sometimes felt like 'projects' instead of 'people'. Whether we were involved in friendship evangelism or discipleship, we had to be willing to share more of our lives and I continued to wrestle with issues of privacy, of time and space, and my independent spirit that accompanied them.

Ayshe, like many Turks, was very intuitive and had uncanny insight into human character. She had been relating to foreigners since her conversion at the age of thirteen and was well aware of our blind spots.

'Why do the foreigners make such a fuss of me and so little of each other?' she asked after a big Christmas party. True, it was tempting to treat the Turkish Christians as 'special' because they really were! In Ankara each believer was literally one in a million. There was great incentive to relate to them because, after all, hadn't God called us to that task? But what about our co-workers – hadn't he called us to them as well?

God was highlighting our need to love one another. We had to learn to express that love with warmth and sincerity to Turk and foreigner alike. Only then would we be seen as disciples of Jesus. Again, it seemed so simple and yet this was really the heart of the matter. If I missed it, no matter how my language progressed and my knowledge of Turkish customs grew, I would be nothing more than a noisy gong or a clashing cymbal.

'How can we Turkish Christians ever be strong if you foreigners never have any problems? You always seem to have it all together and it makes us feel inferior.'

Ayshe was right. We needed the courage to be vulnerable with one another and allow our Turkish brothers and sisters to minister to us. Again it meant opening my life up more to others, confessing weakness and even sin when necessary.

My first visit to a Turkish hairdresser was quite an experience. Ayshe took me to have my long dark hair permed. I had organised a babysitter but the appointment took much longer than I'd expected. After two hours of fussing, the hairdressers all disappeared for lunch, leaving us alone in the salon. I was so worried about being away from my baby so long. It was the first time I'd left her alone with a friend but with my head full of hair curlers there wasn't much I could do about it. As I sat panicking to myself in the mirror, Ayshe took her New Testament from her bag and began happily reading me verses of comfort as she rotated herself playfully in the swivel chair. Usually, I was the one urging her to trust God with her circumstances as some crisis hit her life but this time the roles were reversed and she was enjoying it! We arrived home to find Emma alive and well but a little bewildered to see Mummy looking like a spaniel.

In Turkey it is quite unthinkable to befriend an individual in isolation from their family and friends. A new friendship brings you into that person's *chevre*, a whole circle of relationships, many of which stretch back to childhood. Ayshe's flatmate Hulya became our friend too and would drop in often. For a while she became my language helper. We got to know Granny from the village and Ayshe's younger brother. Then there were lovely times spent with Mum and Dad when they returned from Germany in the summers.

Turks love to pore over photo albums, recalling people and places and reliving experiences together. We introduced our families in this way. It was great for language practice as it involved lots of repetition and helped us learn the Turkish terms used to describe family relationships. For example, the word for 'aunt' depends on which side of the family she belongs. When any of our relatives visited us it brought great joy to our whole *chevre*. It was a relief for the neighbours to see our closeness as they could not understand how we could leave a country and family we said we loved.

My mother came to visit us in Turkey and together with Ayshe we made a trip to Cappadocia. It was only a few hours by car from Ankara and became our favourite place to take friends from the UK. The whole landscape was quite awesome. Volcanic eruptions had resulted in a soft stone covering the area which, being easily worked, had attracted the early monastic communities. The cave-like churches with their Byzantine frescoes were fascinating to explore. Then there were the 'fairy chimneys', long needles of stone, often with large rocks balanced on top. Donkeys laden with provisions wandered up steep, winding paths to cones and pinnacles laced with dwellings and tunnels resembling fairy-tale apartment blocks. Amidst the rock piles were fertile valleys with little farms and orchards.

Ayshe loved Cappadocia and the early church fathers. She felt this was her spiritual heritage. It was during this visit that she told us of her parents' decision to send her abroad for a year of further education. Where should she go and what could she study? It was a great opportunity but she had no desire to carry on studying Economics, her degree subject. All she wanted to study was the Bible. Could we suggest a suitable school in the UK?

As a foreign community of Christian workers we had our own ideas about such things. We had come in order to see an indigenous Turkish church take root and here was a tender plant already desiring to leave. Wouldn't it be better for Muslim converts to have theological training at home within the Turkish context? Students had gone abroad before and not come back! What if Ayshe were to fall in love and marry an Englishman? Some of the finest Turkish Christians in the country at that time did in fact have foreign spouses but there was a feeling that sometime soon the believers would be plentiful and strong enough to begin marrying each other. That would surely be an important stage in church growth. Of course, should Ayshe marry a foreigner she might settle in Britain or some other country altogether. These were all issues that had to be faced.

Thanks to our relationship with Ayshe, our small-minded attitude was challenged again. We realised that she was a precious individual for whose life God had a plan bigger than we could begin to imagine. We couldn't limit his work in her life in order to fit in with our agenda which, from God's perspective, might turn out to be a relatively short-term goal. Rather than try to control her we knew that we must release her to whatever God had in mind.

We encouraged her and the right course was found at a Christian college in Britain. Of course, this step would raise more issues in the years ahead. Ayshe would return with more Biblical knowledge and cultural insight than her male contemporaries. Would there be a role for such a woman – with a developing gift of communication – in the Turkish church? Perhaps she would continue to challenge our preconceptions.

As we picnicked in a vineyard in Cappadocia and opened our lives to one another, a hoopoe flew past. This was the only time I saw one, only once and very briefly. Despite having seen pictures in the bird books, I was surprised and even a little shocked by his size and his beauty. Looking back now on these years in Turkey I realise God had me in an expansion programme! Using cross-cultural issues, he continued to confront my picture of himself, which was far too small and dull. God was so much bigger and more beautiful than I had dreamed possible and his desire would always be to mould me in his image and not the other way round.

4

Mahmut Efendi

Despite the natural warmth of Turkish people, the spiritual climate seemed cold. The military coup of 1980 had brought relief from civil strife and bloodshed, but now, several years later, soldiers continued to have a high profile as they stood guard on street corners, outside schools and government offices dressed for combat, complete with helmets and machine guns. Buses were regularly searched and private cars stopped and checked. For some months curfews restricted visiting and, although the issues were political rather than religious, there was little sense of freedom. The national believers were fearful.

There were sometimes problems with police and rumours of problems, ongoing court cases and the reality of informers. From time to time there would be outraged articles in the newspapers about Western 'tourists' who had been arrested for distributing Christian literature.

This was always interpreted by the authorities as 'Christian propaganda', a heinous term and it usually led to deportation, although it wasn't actually against the law. This sort of publicity in the press caused tensions between the foreign workers and the national believers, and we would distance ourselves from such activities. The result was that we were all highly security conscious. No one wanted to be deported or to get national believers into trouble. Yet surely there were many in the city of Ankara and indeed in the whole of Turkey that the Lord was calling to himself. How could we reach them? Fear was stifling faith. In such an atmosphere what did it mean to serve God and his church?

Blocks of flats in Ankara each had a man who was called the *kapiji*, or literally 'the doorman'. He was a caretaker of sorts who served the building, usually living in a tiny one-roomed accommodation in the basement. These men and their families had often come to the big city from a village outside and being of a lower class were never fully accepted by the folk in the building.

Our *kapiji* was Mahmut. We got to know him through his daughter Sati. She was about four-teen and though she could not speak English at all would bring us her far too difficult English homework. When we visited them, Mahmut was always amazed to hear that in our country there was no one really doing his job. How could we manage without a *kapiji*? Certainly Mahmut was an excellent role model for any would-be missionary who wanted to serve the church, God's building, made from living stones. Mahmut had three basic jobs to do each day.

Most important he had to fire the communal central heating boiler, situated in the basement. Few people realise how cold Ankara and the further eastern parts of Turkey can be in winter. We could have deep snow, and that January of 1985 the temperature was as low as –27°C. It was during this time that our building ran out of coal. For three days we did everything in the one room that we were able to heat with an electric heater. At last coal was delivered at 3 a.m. one morning. As I lay in bed I could hear the load slip from the tip-up truck in the road outside. Our *kapiji* with his pickaxe broke it up small enough to shovel onto his wheelbarrow. Then I heard the squeaky wheel of the barrow as he pushed the load to the coal hatch at the side of the building. Again there was the noise of the coal as it slid through the hatch. This process continued until daylight and by the time we got up the central heating was on and our home was warm again.

God's spiritual building, the church, needed spiritual *kapijis* who would, by praise and prayer, bring the warmth of God's presence, those who would be committed to spiritual warfare, to wrestle through the cold and darkness until the fire of God broke into hearts, engendering faith.

Early each morning Mahmut took his large basket and walked to the local bakery. He would select enough fresh loaves of bread to sell to every flat in the apartment block. Turkish bread is like French bread only the loaves are fatter and shorter. It is the staple diet and a family of four would buy at least four loaves from him. Good housewives would feel the bread to make sure it was really fresh. Turkish bread must be bought daily as it becomes dry and hard quickly.

We had to be people with fresh bread. The Turkish Bible at this time was a big heavy book, last revised around 1880. Since then the Turkish language had changed so much that it was difficult for believers to read it and even harder for those with no knowledge of the Scriptures. A new translation was in progress but would take several more years to complete. Traditional Bible-study materials designed for Christians in the West seldom seemed to hit the mark. Faith had to be relevant and often the questions Turkish friends asked and the issues they were dealing with had to be the basis for study. It was crucial in our situation especially to visit God and his word often so that what we had to offer others was fresh and real, coming from our hearts as well as our heads. Another difference we had to get used to was time orientation. Often interested Turkish friends would miss the planned appointment but turn up when not expected. Our bread had to be fresh at all times.

Every evening Mahmut would come to each door in turn and collect our rubbish. Each family had a bucket with a lid. There were no black plastic bin bags in those days. He would leave the lid on my doorstep to make it easier for himself, then he would take my bucket to a very large bin outside and tip it in. Always he looked at my rubbish. Sometimes he rebuked me if he saw old bread on the top. Bread was far too precious for the bin. It must be placed on a wall outside to be collected for animal feed. Perhaps the crumbs left over from the feeding of the five thousand were gathered up for the same purpose. However, Mahmut never rebuked me for giving him smelly rubbish or too much rubbish. I suppose he knew well what to do with it. He had no intention of keeping it in his little house downstairs or of strewing it all over the stairway. No, it went straight to the big bin outside made for that purpose.

Turkish, we discovered, is a language rich in vocabulary to describe relationships, including broken ones. Family feuds are common and forgiveness is not thought of as a great virtue. It had to be taught and modelled. We had to be those who knew what to do with the sins of others as well as our own, people who would be daily unloading at the cross, God's bin for sin. How much greater our unity would be if we did not harbour the sins of others in our hearts or spread them around his people. There was obviously a place, too, for taking off the lid and confronting one another in truth and love when necessary.

Some efficient *kapijis* could work on extra jobs too. In one apartment our *kapiji* cultivated a garden around the building and in another he and his wife sat outside weaving rugs. Some ran errands throughout the day. However, all these activities were extra. The three main jobs could not be neglected. I began to feel that way about the work we were trying to do as foreign workers from different agencies, all desiring to serve. With every proposed project or programme I found myself asking:

'Are the three basic jobs being done?'

This servant–leadership model turns the notion of hierarchy on its head. Mahmut's role was important but his place was small – just one room in the basement. It reminded me that our job was more about supporting and under-girding from below than lording it from above.

However, being a *kapiji* had privileges as well as responsibilities. Mahmut's place may have been small yet its location, right next to the boiler, made it the hottest home in the whole building. Likewise, if we were willing to put time and effort into praise and prayer on behalf of God's people, our own hearts would be ablaze with his Spirit.

Mahmut knew the baker well, because he went to him every day for bread. They were on first-name terms. If we made it our business to receive the Word of God daily for ourselves and others, we would get to know God, the living Word, very much better.

A *kapiji* was a humble man. There was nothing glamorous about his job, which dealt with the basics of life. Every day he had to carry buckets of smelly rubbish to the bin. Frequent visits to the Cross, unloading sin, would keep us real with ourselves and save us from pride.

The *kapiji* had keys for the main door of the apartment block. Perhaps God was looking for true servants like Mahmut to whom he could entrust the keys of his building, the church.

5

Hold the Baby

Huseyin and Fatma had arrived late. The long bumpy journey from the outskirts of the city had left Fatma travel-sick. They only came about once a month but the trip was always a trial for Fatma and she lay down on our bed.

The meeting had started. Turkish hymns, all set in a minor key, filled the lounge. Pam, our American co-worker and music major, accompanied on the *saz*, a guitar-like Turkish instrument.

Before rejoining the group, I neatened the clutter of shoes in our narrow hallway. Samim, almost ten months old, straddled my hip. Since his birth the previous summer of 1984, I had become amazed at how many jobs I could do with one hand. His colic was improving, though he was still often wakeful at night. Today, he was just plain miserable and I put it down to teething.

The green plastic slip-on shoes belonged to Anush, an old Armenian believer. Her husband

Sergis had recently come to faith and, as usual, they had arrived early. We were supposed to meet at two o'clock but, having a different concept of time, this old couple would rise with the sun, catch a bus and come. Their return fares were wrapped in a piece of cloth tucked in Anush's clothing. In her hand she carried a raffia shopping bag full of brightly knitted dolls and pot holders that she hoped to sell to the gathering.

Fortunately, our friend Ayshe had also arrived early. Emma loved Ayshe and while they had all chatted together, I had tidied up the bedrooms and got organised for the afternoon tea that we would share as a fellowship at the end of the meeting. This had involved setting out about thirty tiny tea glasses with saucers and spoons in the kitchen, and a similar number of tea plates with cake and a savoury snack on each. Covering it over with a nylon cloth, I had returned to the lounge to serve lunch.

Lunch had been simple: just lentil soup, bread, white goats' cheese and tomatoes.

'Don't you ever eat meat?' Sergis asked.

Poor Sergis! I knew he and Anush would never have money for meat and I feared he had expected something better from the 'foreigners'.

The white tennis shoes belonged to Mohammed, an Azeri Turk from Iran, studying at the Middle East Technical University. He had been

sent to the United States to study naval engineering but, due to the American hostage crisis
of 1981, had been forced to leave and continue
his studies in Ankara. Living in a cheap hotel in
town, he met an Iranian Christian Jew who
introduced him to Jesus and then moved on. For
a while he called himself Mark, embarrassed to
be a Christian with such a Muslim name but as
he grew in the Lord he felt comfortable to be
Mohammed again!

Huseyin, number two, had left his socks
inside his shoes. He reckoned they smelled
worse than his feet! He'd also left one of his
wooden crutches leaning against the wall. Crip-
pled due to a vaccination error in childhood, he
had learned to walk with crutches when he was
seven. His mind was sharp. He loved chess and
regularly beat our computer program. His face
was full of character and he could win any argument with words. Huseyin and his friends had
long since rejected Islam and were heavily
involved in left-wing politics. We soon discovered that witnessing for Christ was not neces-
sarily a sign of spiritual growth. No! Huseyin
loved to outsmart his Muslim teachers with
ammunition acquired at the Bible study. Today
he'd brought his taxi-driver friend Mesut whose
smart black shoes had obviously been polished
for the occasion by the shoeshine boys.

The bell rang. It was Hamdi and his family.
They all needed a drink of water after the long

bus trip but I had no water at all. We hadn't had tap water for five days and my drinking-water bottle was empty. The little girls and Kesban joined the other children and two American friends for Sunday School in the children's bedroom. Kesban found it hard to sit through a meeting. As I passed our bedroom the Dutch lady was in beside Fatma, feeding her baby. Fatma felt better and they were having a good chat sitting on the bed together.

The group in the lounge had moved into a time of prayer. Orhan was reciting from the book of Romans. He was a middle-aged civil servant who had been a devout Muslim. In his search for truth he had experienced the various sects in Islam, finding little satisfaction. As a boy growing up in eastern Turkey he had often wandered among ruins of Christian times and wondered if God had changed. One evening many years later he tuned into TransWorld Radio by accident, and heard the Bible being read for the first time in his life. He knew this was God's word and through the radio contact was linked up with the believers in Ankara. Orhan had great problems with his wife who, though she softened a little over the years, burnt his Bible and notebook many times. It was now his most treasured possession and he memorised and recited it at every opportunity. After half an hour the Dutchman leading the meeting quietly suggested we had had enough.

Later, Orhan explained he had planned to recite for an hour!

Chichek, the wife of the dustman, Huseyin number three, asked for an aspirin for her headache and followed me out to the kitchen. Ayshe's flatmate Hulya was smoking a cigarette on the balcony.

Suddenly, the shout of '*Suju, suju,*' was heard in the street below. In an instant I was leaning over the railing yelling the number of our apartment. It was the water lorry but I wasn't sure if I had been noticed. So many were calling to him. Drinking water was delivered weekly to our area. Many like us used tap water for cleaning and cooking but preferred to buy spring water for drinking. However, this five-day cut in supply meant that the people who were usually content to drink tap water were also trying to buy from the *suju*. The demand for his attention was so much greater than normal, I would be lucky to get a bottle.

I heard his feet on the stair. ' Hold the baby,' I cried, handing Samim to Hulya and carrying our large plastic water container to the front door. The water slurped from his bottle to mine. It felt beautifully cold against my legs as I manoeuvred it back to its place in the kitchen. With my dipper I filled up a jug and a kettle and felt I was in business again.

Samim needed changing but I had so few clean nappies left. The bucket in the bathroom was full to overflowing. Each day I had hoped for water but it hadn't come. A well had been opened in the school playground nearby but the queues were so long and the nappies were so many…

Back in the lounge the meeting continued with testimonies, a message and more prayer. Anush asked prayer for her eyes as she was finding knitting difficult. Ayshe suggested she might need glasses as she was getting older. No one, including Anush, knew her age exactly. It was agreed that the fellowship would pay and Orhan, who called her Mother, would take her to an optician.

As the tea glasses went back and forth from the kitchen the children played with all the toys everywhere. By six o'clock the house looked as if a bomb had hit it. People began to leave in ones and twos. A mass exodus would attract too much attention. Ayshe, Hulya and Mohammed wanted to talk more and so we went to our favourite tea garden. It was so good to walk out in the summer evening. Samim was happy at last to ride in his pushchair and then to watch the giant goldfish swimming in the ornamental pond. Emma, as usual, was fussed over by the waiters and we all enjoyed drinking tea from our samovar and eating *gozleme,* a kind of thin savoury pancake filled with cheese and parsley. When we came home we were really tired and there was still the tidying-up to do.

As a fellowship we were growing. It was something of a joke that we now had three Huseyins in our group and therefore they had to be identified by occupation, as well as forename. Surnames are not commonly used in Turkey when referring to people. Including children, we often numbered more than twenty on a Sunday. It had been an answer to prayer when contact with a Catholic priest had led to our being allowed to use the Vatican Embassy Chapel for our meetings. However, that had not lasted long. The police had put pressure on the Vatican and we were asked to leave. We were back meeting in foreign homes.

Noone felt this situation was ideal and sometimes the burden of it all seemed too great. We longed for the Turkish church to be indigenous, to meet on Turkish soil and be led by local brothers. As foreigners we were committed to working with our contacts within their families and natural relationships, but family opposition and fear of hostility from conservative neighbourhoods didn't make it easy for us or our Turkish friends.

It was, therefore, an odd assortment of people in the fellowship, who naturally had little in common with one another. Often we wondered if the group would survive if we foreigners were all forced to leave. Were we supposed to be carrying it to such an extent?

Yet, in a sense it was a baby church and just

as a tiny baby has all the potential to grow into the mature person so this baby church perhaps embodied God's vision for the whole country. A devout Muslim man converted and calling an old Armenian believer 'Mother', Kurd and Turk calling each other 'Sister', political left and right, old and young, educated and illiterate worshipping God together. No doubt, the future Turkish church would have many varied expressions throughout the country but this was the baby and had to encompass all.

I remembered the difficulties we'd had after the birth of our own first baby, Emma. She was rushed back into hospital with a high fever and lay naked in what seemed like an enormous metal cot with a drip running into her head. I wasn't allowed to feed her in case I dislodged the drip and was warned to hold her very carefully indeed.

The days were filled with painful tests – only three days but they seemed like an eternity. I paced up and down the hospital room like a sentry on duty, praying life into her little body and daring death to come near. Now I was kneeling surrendering her to God, then with outstretched arms I was praising and singing over the bed. On the third day I heard the powerful hymn, 'Great is thy faithfulness' come wafting along the corridor from the programme *Songs of Praise* in the TV lounge. The doctor announced we could go home and an explanation for the fever was never given.

As I thought of my own baby's early days of life, I began to hear God asking me if I was willing to help 'hold' his baby church. Yes, the feeding was unnatural but the baby was still struggling to live. She was tiny and vulnerable and painful tests were coming one after the other. But it would only be for 'three days'.

I realised God's heart towards this small group of people in a new way and felt ashamed. There had been a sense of urgency and passion in my prayers for my own child. What did God feel for his? Again, it seemed prayer was the main support he was asking of me and an attitude that held with care, not in a grasping, possessive way but always open to God, remembering the baby was his.

'Yes, God, I'm willing,' I said, 'But I can't do it without water. I feel so dry. I need more of your Spirit, Lord.'

As we lay in bed that night we heard the glad sound of gurgling in the pipes. God was faithful and my thoughts turned to the nappy bucket waiting for me in the morning.

6

A Spacious Place

I sat in the living room. We had moved to this flat when our landlord had sold our previous home. The new landlady had made a point of emphasising the thickness of the walls. Certainly it was comforting to know there was good soundproofing when we gathered to sing. However, the room was an odd shape – very long and narrow – and it was becoming a bit tight when we met together.

It seemed to me as I sat there that it resembled my heart – tight, narrow with very thick walls. There didn't seem to be enough room for the people we were supposed to love. Often I felt resentful sharing my home and my family with so many people. What could I do to 'expand the place of my tent', 'stretch out the pegs' so to speak?

'Sell all you have!' was Jesus' command to the rich young ruler. A dose of extravagant giving was his remedy for the materialistic heart. Perhaps for mine it would be a dose of extravagant loving.

Now, there was a brother in the fellowship in a very difficult situation. Ayhan was a Turkish student from Northern Cyprus. His father, who was in the government there, had disowned him because of his faith and stopped all his money. He had just had a painful operation to straighten his club feet but where would he go after being discharged from hospital? Perhaps this was my opportunity to voluntarily go an extra mile.

We partitioned our long narrow living room to accommodate Ayhan. His feet were so painful that he couldn't stand without help. Everything had to be done for him including taking him to the bathroom. Yet, having him to live with us was much easier than we had anticipated. We all loved him. Of course, now we had his visitors as well as our own and the house was busy from morning until night. However, instead of being conscious of the extra work, I was more aware of extra helpers.

After a few months, our Dutch friends and the American *saz* player, Pam, were all deported. They'd been involved with a girl who had come to faith. Her relationship with her father had never been good and this was the last straw. He complained to the police and our three friends were given until the end of the month to leave the country.

With heavy hearts the family returned to Holland and a work amongst Turks in Rotterdam, but Pam decided to try to re-enter the country on a tourist visa. She felt uneasy about coming back to the same house and so, just a week before Christmas 1987, Pam moved to our home and we moved to the Dutch family's house, together with Ayhan, whose feet had healed and who had returned to university.

Of course we missed Wolter and Ine and their children. We had grown to love them over the years as friends, not just co-workers. Such partings were never easy and would be repeated as time went on.

Our new flat was indeed a spacious place with a large lounge ideal for meetings. There was a room we could use as a study and also a guest room for Ayhan. It was the first time we had had a garden area around our apartment building where the children could ride their bikes, and, much to their delight, a low balcony which made it possible to get to know the neighbourhood cats. They all lived out of dustbins in the area and Emma enjoyed giving them names. Our escapades with the semi-wild cats of Turkey were to be many over the years, and they began here with our balcony, which quickly became one of their regular 'hangouts'.

First, there was Debbie, unable to walk due to pellet wounds in her legs, who spent a few days with us recuperating. Next, there was Blackie, unable to eat due to a large chicken bone which had become wedged across his mouth. Buster received prayer and recovered from a chest infection, and then there was the night we dealt with Puffin.

Julyan's Uncle Denys, a Professor in Aeronautical Engineering and a keen Christian, came to Ankara University as a visiting lecturer. Suat, a new believer and close friend, was a student of the same department. We arranged a meeting in our home for Uncle Denys to talk about 'Science and Faith'. Many students came and soon there was a lively discussion with Julyan helping as interpreter.

As I left the room to prepare tea for everyone, the doorbell rang and there was the *kapiji* holding a cat that he'd found in a barrel of whitewash. He dropped her amidst the many pairs of shoes, dripping paint everywhere.

There was nothing I could do with so many people in the house. I shut her in the little toilet and Emma stood guard. We quickly wiped all the shoes and, at midnight when everyone had gone, we filled the old plastic baby bath and washed a very grateful cat. Fortunately, Uncle Denys and Auntie Rosemary love cats. For them it all added to the blessing of the evening.

Soon after moving into our 'spacious place' we had a phone call from Iran. Our friend Mohammed who'd graduated and returned there, had married a Muslim convert girl against his parents' wishes. Their wedding had been secret and they were literally 'on the run' from his father's violent threats. Could they take a bus to Ankara and stay with us for a while?

In our new flat we had room. We exchanged the bunkbeds in the guest room for a double bed, ready for the honeymoon couple and Ayhan moved into the study. Mohammed and Golnaz arrived – happy to be with us. Communication was difficult. Of course, they spoke Farsi with each other and we spoke Turkish or English with Mohammed. Golnaz, however, didn't come from the Azeri Turkish-speaking part of the country and had never learned English. She was dreadfully homesick.

Their visas would expire in three months. What should they do? Where should they go? We prayed and made lots of phone calls. Old American friends of Mohammed, who had previously lived in Ankara, were now in Australia, reaching out to Turks. Perhaps they could help. What about the Iranian fellowship in London? Maybe there was a possibility of asylum in England. Should they try to find a way to stay longer in Ankara? Due to the Iran-Iraq war, many Iranians had fled to Turkey as refugees. Could Mohammed and Golnaz help to begin a work among them? After two months of prayerful heart-searching, Mohammed and Golnaz knew their place was back in Iran. They decided to return and live in Golnaz's city near her family who were more favourable towards the marriage.

Meanwhile, there was a growing sense of urgency around Ayhan's situation. His visa, without which he couldn't continue at university, had expired. As a fellowship we prayed. A church leader from another city, himself a Cypriot, volunteered to visit his father and act as go-between. This offer was rejected by Ayhan.

Spiritually, we knew things were not right but we put it down to the rejection he had known due to his handicap and his present family pressure. A Korean brother took the initiative to visit his professor and to our horror discovered that there was no such student as Ayhan at the university. When we confronted him, his reaction was one of angry outrage and as Julyan and Hanwoo tried to talk to him he gathered his belongings and stormed out into the dark rainy night.

Everyone was deeply shocked. It was hard to believe that our Turkish friends, as well as ourselves, had been taken in by his story. We later discovered that he was not even Cypriot but came from a small town outside Ankara. It was a bitter disappointment. We had all loved and given so much but it had been returned by hatred. We felt betrayed. He had lived with us for seven months yet we didn't really know him. We needed so much more discernment. The Lord was kind and comforted us with the example of Judas whom Jesus discipled for three years although he knew what was in his mind.

I had asked God to expand my heart. I had wanted more love but as I felt the pain I discovered that the spacious place was not about love in quantity but in quality. Yes, we needed more discernment, to trust our hunches and pray more seriously when doubts nagged, but love would always be vulnerable and open to abuse.

It was good to be able to share our sadness with our dear friend Mohammed. Before returning to Iran he decided to telephone his own family to find out their feelings towards him. He spoke to his mother.

'Come home, son,' she urged. 'Your father has forgiven you. Bring Golnaz for Iranian New Year. We want to give her the gold jewellery that we should have given her at the wedding.'

How wonderful it was to experience Mohammed's joy as he anticipated the reunion with his father. We longed that Ayhan would know, likewise, reconciliation with his Father in Heaven.

7

Move a Mountain

Japanese scientists in the rooftop restaurant of downtown Ankara were discussing the chronic air pollution problem. As they looked out over the city, they were heard to declare:

'The answer is to move a mountain!'

Ankara sits in a basin surrounded by mountains. There is rarely any wind to lift the smog. On our first New Year's Day we had climbed one of them expecting a great view from the top only to look down upon thick polluted clouds.

It was quite common, especially for the children, to cough their way through the winter. This year was no exception and one February night they were both distressed. Samim had spluttered out his dummy and I couldn't find it. Emma was panicking, feeling she couldn't catch her breath. It was past midnight and I decided to phone Melih's house to see if Julyan would be home soon.

Melih was the drummer of a rock band. He had come to the Lord through the correspondence course and had introduced us to his circle of friends. He lived with his brother Osman, the lead singer, and Julyan had gone to visit them.

With the sound of crying children in my ears I made my call. 'Well,' said Julyan, 'I'll come if you really need me, but Osman is just about to pray to Jesus.'

What could I say? Life seemed so hard. And yet if Osman came to faith, it would all be worthwhile.

'Okay,' I uttered quickly, 'We'll manage,' and we did!

Osman believed that night and what a joy it was to study the newly completed translation of the New Testament with them. We were so glad to have a modern version of Scripture to give to these modern Turkish young men. A similar project to translate the Old Testament was under way but it would be another ten years, at least, until we had the whole Word of God in a language readily understood by modern Turks.

Their mother had a dream about Jesus and became open and supportive. Osman began writing songs and they decided to put on a concert. Financially, it was a disaster but it was thrilling to see a Turkish heavy metal version of 'The Lord's my Shepherd' and two more of their circle come to believe in Jesus.

Now, a retreat had been planned for the
Christian workers in Turkey. I was really
looking forward to it – a weekend in a hotel
with no practical jobs to do – just fellowship
with God and each other. I had even arranged
for Harriet, a Dutch girl who was visiting as a
short-term worker to come and supervise the
children so that the Mums would get a break
and receive much-needed ministry.

These annual get-togethers were always
special. Turkey is a big country and we didn't
see workers from other cities often. It was
always a great time of mutual encouragement
and I expected to hear from God. Maybe we
would all sense his directing, giving us fresh
vision and, oh, the freedom to speak English, to
understand fully and be more fully understood,
even for a weekend.

Alas, that winter the doctor confirmed that
despite their vaccinations the coughs were not
the usual variety but whooping cough itself.
The children and I would be staying at home.

As the hotel was in a town not too far from
Ankara a couple from Istanbul, who were going
to travel with us, had come to stay for a few
days. Though my inside ached with disappointment, I managed to remain cheerful just
long enough to wave them all goodbye. Even
then there was no time for self-pity as the children's condition deteriorated that evening.
Samim slept with me and I moved Emma's

mattress beside my bed so that I could reach them both easily in the night. Emma was now vomiting with her coughing attacks and Samim just cried and cried and couldn't sleep.

When at last they dozed off the sense of disappointment quite overwhelmed me. Why did I feel so dejected? What was really bothering me deep down? When I was honest I had to admit that I found it hard to believe God didn't want me there. Didn't he need me there? In fact, how could he have such a retreat without me?

The telephone rang. It was Melih. Although it was after midnight, it was not late for him. 'Lenna, Abla (big sister), can you give me a verse from the Bible that I can read together with my friend?' My mind was blank. I was so tired I couldn't even muster a John 3:16. Instead, I blurted out 'Psalm 63' and returned and lay down on my bed.

'Psalm 63,' I repeated to myself. What made me say it? I couldn't even remember which psalm it was. I reached for my Bible and began reading and, of course, found God was speaking. I found a God 'who was with me through the watches of the night' as I lay on my bed and who 'upheld me with his right hand'. I found a God whose love was better than retreats or conferences and a God who seemed to want me all to himself. Yes, he wanted me just where I was. As my soul had thirsted and my body longed for him in my weary land, I found myself in the sanctuary beholding his power and glory.

The next day and night I was able to appreciate the privilege of being close to my children and the bonding that comes through such times together. When Julyan and the others returned both Emma and Samim were feeling much better. I was eager to know how the retreat had gone. What had been the mood? Had God spoken? Had the workers been challenged, envisioned?

News had come of police problems in Adana where a couple, Chris and Lily, had been unable to renew their residence permits and were having to return to Canada. Spiritually, the pressure was increasing. Hardship and suffering were coming but God would be with us. He would uphold us with his right hand.

I smiled inwardly as I realised I had just lived through a preview of things to come. Perhaps through hardship and suffering God would develop an intimacy with us all that would produce perseverance and character. A deeper dependence on God and each other would reveal the strength of his love, and a greater trust in his purposes would engender fresh hope.

God would grow in us a faith to move mountains – mountains of fear and unbelief that so hindered the wind of his Spirit. How we needed that cleansing wind to lift the smog that makes people blind to the truth and reality of Jesus.

8

Darkness to Light

News came of arrests in Samsun, a town on the Black Sea coast. A foreign brother and two nationals had gone against advice and received large amounts of money to print and distribute evangelistic literature by mail. An address book belonging to one of them provided police with the names of believers around the country – and the round-up began.

In Ankara we wondered when our time would come. Then, one Sunday morning Julyan's name featured in an article in a popular national newspaper which accused him of poisoning Turkey's youth. Apparently, he organised camps at which he offered young men money and foreign women if they converted to Christianity. My first reaction was one of fear. What would the neighbours think? Would they believe the lies? As I prepared breakfast, it felt as though I were wading through treacle. We lay low that day, spending a nostalgic afternoon in our favourite tea garden, looking back over our years in Ankara and considering what we would do after being deported! Despite their anxieties, the Turkish believers continued to meet together and, as the days passed, continued to visit us in our home, even the very new believers. Previous scares like this had scattered and wiped out the flock, but times were changing. We were growing in number and strength.

Elif, whose parents had been immigrants from Estonia, had come to faith. Knowing her roots to be Christian, she had contacted the correspondence course in order to learn more and pass it on to her family. Her teenage daughter and four younger children believed, followed by her three step-sisters, their children, a Muslim brother-in-law and his brother. Many other relatives were touched. A real community was developing and with it a growing sense of identity for the Turkish church.

The arrival of Christians from South Korea also helped to strengthen us. Turks and Koreans both trace their ancestry to Mongolian tribes from Central Asia. Their grammar and culture have similarities and we envied the speed with which our new co-workers learnt the language. South Koreans also feel indebted to Turkey, whose soldiers showed such heroism fighting against Communism in the Korean war. Most important, the South Koreans came with their

experience of massive church growth at home
and helped to boost our faith level.

We were now meeting in one of the class-
rooms of a school linked to the German
Embassy, thanks to the contacts of Barbara, a
German co-worker. Although we were safely
meeting on Embassy grounds, we would sing
our favourite song, 'Fear not for I am with you',
with one eye on the road outside. We waited
nervously as the days passed and news continued to filter through of harassment in other
cities.

The knock on our door finally came on 21st
March 1988, a full three weeks after the
damning newspaper article had been published. We were not too surprised when the
plain-clothes policeman on our doorstep
invited Julyan to come with him for a 'chat'. He
picked up his jacket and went off, giving me a
shrug of his shoulders as if to say, 'I don't know
if this chat will last hours, days or weeks?'
Immediately, I began phoning round and discovered that Julyan was not the only one.
Twelve believers in Ankara had been taken for
interrogation, of whom seven were foreigners and
five were Turks. The wife of one of the men had
overheard the police planning a house search.

All evening I felt anxious and decided not to
go to bed. Emma and Samim were asleep. They
had been so good. I had explained that Daddy
was at the police station because the police

wanted to know about the church and what we all believed about God. That had satisfied them for now but I wondered what I would say as time went on. It was comforting for the children to know that Daddy was with such good friends who would be able to help him answer any difficult questions. The knowledge that the believers were together comforted me too. I was glad the Turkish Christians were not alone in their suffering and hoped that having foreigners amongst them would ensure better treatment, limiting their ordeal.

Two plain-clothes policemen arrived around midnight. It was such a relief to see Julyan with them when I opened the door, and to find that they only wanted to search the study. They decided to take away the books from the bookcase and asked for an empty suitcase. Together we tutted and threw back our heads in Turkish style to signal a negative response. Our suitcases were far from empty – they were full of Turkish New Testaments and Christian books and were sitting on shelves hidden in a curtained recess in the hall! It wasn't that having them was against the law but they were too precious for us to allow them to be confiscated.

In the end they emptied a small metal trunk of Julyan's tools, packed it with books from the study and carried it out through the hall like a coffin. As they passed the recess, the curtain was caught by one of the policeman's shoulders but, fortunately, they didn't notice what lay behind. Before leaving, Julyan collected ointment for his eczema, which was always worse under stress, and a sweater because the nights were cold. He had no idea how long they would be in the cells. In Turkey it is possible to be held for two weeks without being charged.

When they all left I was amazed at the peace God had given me, which was in stark contrast to the fear I'd experienced earlier. Joy quite overwhelmed me and I was filled with praise and prayer, confident that God was going to use this situation in his purpose for the church. It was liberating to feel part of a plan that was bigger than myself. A new tape of a Scottish singer/songwriter, Ian White, had just arrived from relatives in Scotland. The words of Psalm 40 rang out:

'Many will see, many will fear and many will put their trust in the Lord.'

There had been a case in Gaziantep in the east where Turkish believers had suffered torture alone. One young man had cried out to God, 'Why?' In answer to his plight the Lord seemed to say:

'The human authorities and the spiritual principalities must see that there are Turkish people who are willing to suffer for my name.'

In Ankara it was a privilege to be with the national Christians. There was much mutual encouragement outside the cells, where we as relatives and friends felt our bond deepen. Being together inside the cells also greatly strengthened the believers and helped them to hold on to their faith. Ayshe was the first woman to be picked up. She was in a cramped cell feeling very alone and afraid, especially as the police were in the next room and there was a big hole in the partitioning wall. The cell was so narrow that she dared not lie down on the floor, or even sit down and risk falling asleep. She struggled to stay awake on her feet with her eyes fixed firmly on the menacing hole. Poor Ayshe, she was so tired. Just as she was feeling desperate, the door opened and in came Elif, a larger older woman.

'Don't worry,' said Elif. 'I'll lie down and block the hole and you can lie next to me. But be careful I don't roll over on top of you in the middle of the night and photocopy you flat!'

This story brought great hilarity after the ordeal was over and was told and re-told. Hard though the experience was, we learned that fellowship through suffering brings an intimacy that comes no other way.

At home the children continued to cope well. Emma at this time was attending the school attached to the British Embassy on the other side of the city. One fear I had was of being suddenly separated from the children, when their father had already disappeared. My protective mothering instinct probably went into overdrive and I kept Emma from school until the crisis was past. They understood that if Daddy was helping the police to read our books it might take a while. Samim suggested that we take his books along as they had pictures. I think he thought that might simplify things and hasten Daddy's homecoming. On the third day an unshaven Julyan appeared unexpectedly. They had been charged and released pending trial.

We learned something more about the power of prayer during this time. Phone calls came from all over – from South Korea, from Italy, from the USA, from the UK, all confirming a worldwide network of prayer. One day Julyan had felt so aware of being upheld in prayer that he was quite overcome with emotion. We discovered that at these crucial times, God has his intercessors and his troubleshooters.

One such man was Luther! Unknown to any of us, this elderly German gentleman with his long grey beard and belted raincoat had arrived in Ankara on the day of the arrests. He had donned a sandwich-board and had been picked up by the police while parading his verses and giving out tracts in the city centre. Orhan, the fellowship bookkeeper had been picked up first and as he recalled that day, he told us:

'I felt very fearful as I was led to the interrogation room. Sitting on a bench in the corridor was an old man in what seemed to me an attitude of prayer. In my spirit I knew he was my brother and that I was not alone.'

When the believers were released pending trial, Luther had nowhere to stay and moved in with our English friend, John. However, he was determined to finish giving out his tracts and was repeatedly picked up and then released at John's request. It was hard to explain to Luther that the real problem was that his tracts had been printed in Germany and had not passed Turkish censorship. They were illegal!

Eventually, the police became exasperated and had him deported before the trial took place. I went to the bus station to wave him off. There he was, sitting next to a plain-clothes policeman, whose job it was to escort him to the Greek border. They looked like a teacher and student, as Luther studied his German Bible and referred the policeman to verses in the Turkish New Testament that he had given him. The journey would take about twelve hours, and I wondered if he would be a Christian by the end.

One evening before Luther left, we gathered to pray. There were many issues to bring to the Lord: the court case scheduled for May, our need for a suitable lawyer and an honest, favourable judge; then of course, there was the future of the church in Ankara and Turkey.

As we were worshipping the Lord, Luther, with great deliberation, stood to his feet. With hands clasped tightly together and eyes earnestly closed, he prayed in slow, staccato tones:

'Lord, I pray for this dark country.'

On the word 'dark' the lights went out and we were plunged into blackness. Now, power cuts were not so unusual but this was no ordinary one. As I lit the candles we all knew that we must pray until the lights returned. And so we began to pray against every kind of darkness in Turkey that we could think of. We prayed against fear, violence, lies, corruption, injustice, materialism, greed, immorality, pornography – but still no light. We tried another round adding a few more evils to our list. Still no light!

Then a Swedish brother ventured:

'I feel sick and the verse that is coming to my mind is from Revelation 3, "If you are neither hot nor cold I will spew you out of my mouth".'

There was silence as God turned his searchlight on our hearts. In repentance a simple prayer was heard:

'Oh, Lord, please let us shine for you.'

As the word 'shine' was prayed, the lights returned. We all saw in a new way that God's answer to the darkness of our world was the light of his people. He seemed so much more concerned about the brightness in us than the darkness out there. That night our commitment to be the light that scatters and overcomes was strengthened and we determined with God by his grace to live in his love, keeping short accounts so that the sins we'd prayed about would not cast their shadow across our hearts.

9

The Barbed Wire Fence

Week by week as we waited for the trial, we continued to meet in the German school, but we gathered in homes afterwards for tea and for special occasions. Our house with its spacious lounge was great for parties. At Easter we had around fifty people for a pot-luck meal and evangelistic drama.

Katie, the cat, came to live with us. She was the runt of her litter and decided to follow us home one day. She grew to be a big stripy tabby, enjoying access to the garden via our low balcony. We inserted a cat flap in our kitchen door which greatly intrigued our visitors.

The garden area was also enjoyed by the children. They loved to go outside and ride all around the building. One day as I carried out their little bikes, they ran on ahead of me. Now there was a project to have a small patch of grass and a fountain in the garden among some trees. Grass doesn't grow easily in Turkey and, in order to guard the area, a length of barbed wire was stretched around it, about the height of a toddler.

Samim ventured under the wire to take a look at the fountain but, startled by someone banging on the window, ran quickly out catching his face as he went. There seemed to be blood everywhere. The cut had just missed his eye. Once inside I managed to stop the bleeding and after a cuddle he fell asleep. The wire was new and his tetanus injections were up to date. It was a Sunday evening and Julyan was out of town. There was a clinic down the road but I hated to add to the stress if it wasn't necessary. Emma suggested we pray and turn the mirror round so he wouldn't remember when he woke up. That's just what we did and it worked. Samim, however, was left with a scar.

Though the grass grew and the fountain was completed the wire remained for almost a year. It became symbolic to me of our spiritual situation. There were people in Turkey searching for the fountain of life, Jesus himself, but in order to reach him they must come through a barbed wire fence of opposition that left many inwardly scarred.

The interrogation during those days in the cells highlighted the kind of problems Turks have with Christianity. Repeatedly the police accused the Turkish believers of being traitors to their country. They repeated the common dictum that 'To be a Turk is to be a Muslim.' 'You have joined the enemies of the people,' they shouted. To be told, 'The nation has lost you,' or 'You don't belong here anymore,' was deeply hurtful for the believers, who loved their country as much as anyone.

All through their history the Turks have had enemies who called themselves 'Christian'. When the Turkish tribes arrived in Anatolia from Central Asia, they faced the first Crusade, an army raised up by the Pope and sent to recapture Jerusalem and its holy sites from the Muslims. On the way to Jerusalem, these so-called 'Christian knights' massacred Jews, sacked the Greek Orthodox churches of Constantinople and perpetrated ghastly atrocities against Muslims. All over the Middle East the Crusades are keenly remembered as an example of Christian militarism, and so the cross that was emblazoned on the crusaders' shields is seen not as a symbol of love and self-sacrifice, but as a symbol of violence and aggression. To this day Turks see Christian activity, whether Serbs shelling Bosnian Muslims in Sarajevo or missionaries distributing New Testaments in Istanbul, as a resurgence of the 'Crusader spirit'.

Julyan asked the policeman interrogating him why the police were expending so much energy in harassing a tiny group of harmless

Christians, when there were far more sinister terrorist groups out east, setting off bombs and causing mayhem. The answer was that although we were small now, if we grew in size we would cause Turkish society to be divided between Muslim and Christian, and as a result Turkey would suffer a horrific civil war like Lebanon. As far as the police were concerned we had a Western political agenda, to divide and conquer Turkey. In fact, they had a strong suspicion that we were directed and funded by the CIA.

Another cause of mistrust and prejudice were religious misunderstandings. Every Turkish child is taught in school that the New Testament has been changed to remove references to the coming of God's final prophet, Mohammed. In AD 325 a church council was held in Nicaea, now Iznik near Istanbul, to discuss the deity of Christ. Turkish school books say this council was held because so many spurious gospels were being produced, and out of the pile of counterfeits they decided Matthew, Mark, Luke and John were the real ones.

Another common misunderstanding is Jesus' title 'Son of God'. The Koran itself says that this means that God took a partner and had sex, which resulted in the birth of a son – something it sees as offensive and blasphemous as we do. However, as a result, Turks think

Christians believe that God the Father had sexual intercourse with Mary.

Indeed, the respect and adoration given to Mary by the traditional Orthodox and Catholic communities living in the Middle East have led Muslims to assume that Christians worship her, and that our Trinity consists of Father, Son and Mother Mary. The Eastern Orthodox Christians, who have struggled to survive centuries of Muslim pressure, worship in gloriously decorated church buildings, full of incense and surrounded by icons. To the watching Muslims, all this praying to pictures looks like idolatry, and stands in stark contrast to the pious simplicity of their mosques. Christians are idolaters!

Despite all this, the believers had stood well through their time inside prison, refusing to deny their faith while sharing their simple testimonies. There had been much prayer and the support of being together.

As we anticipated the court case, there was considerable debate about which lawyer to choose. One possibility was a famous expensive name, experienced in defending the Jehovah's Witnesses. Or we could choose Fatih, a brand new lawyer and family friend. He had been in Julyan's English class and had already helped us a little unofficially. We often felt like David up against Goliath, and as we considered his victory we remembered David's faith in God, but also that he used the giant's own sword to cut off his head. Surely our sword was Turkey's own secular constitution which guaranteed freedom of religion. It was decided that Fatih should wield it.

When the day of the trial finally arrived, our Dutch friend Harriet offered to babysit to allow me to go to court too. The atmosphere was electric. Everyone felt bathed in prayer. Even the BBC unwittingly helped by broadcasting a pre-recorded interview with Julyan at seven o'clock in the morning, British time, producing another cloud of intercession at exactly nine o'clock Turkish time as we were arriving at the court house.

Would Turkey uphold its constitution? The police had given Orhan, the fellowship book-keeper a hard time. They were sure his finance notebook was coded, as the amounts registered were so small. However, we were delighted with the judge, who added positive comments when dictating the defendants' statements to the court clerk. He concluded that the believers were in no way making financial gain from their faith. This had been the charge – article 6187, a law originally designed to inhibit the activities of fundamentalist Muslims!

The hearing had taken less than an hour, but noone wanted to leave. We hung around chatting over tea and praising God for his goodness. The atmosphere amongst us resembled that of a wedding   party,   which   seemed   quite incongruous among soldiers carrying machine-guns and less fortunate prisoners being led around in chains. God was doing something very special for us and we all felt it.

As we arrived home, Samim came running to meet us.

'Mummy, Mummy,' he cried, 'Come and see, come and see.'

He led me by the hand out to the kitchen balcony.

'Look!' he squealed, 'They've taken away the barbed wire fence'.

Tears of joy streamed down my cheeks. Yes, it really was gone. I knew we'd somehow broken through the fear barrier – the mountain had taken a mighty blow. His Spirit would move now as never before and God had taken a horrid personal experience – the scarring of my son – and filled it with meaning.

Of course, there were further battles. In September of the same year, the Ankara believers, including Julyan, were arrested again and held for a week in the basement of the police head-quarters. I was coming back from a visit to Scotland with the children and wondered if our plane might pass Julyan's in the sky! Thankfully, he had been released that afternoon and was there to greet our arrival at Ankara airport. The purpose this time had been mere harass-ment and, though it had been nasty, no charges had been brought.

The serious investigation, which had resulted in a court case and subsequent acquittal, had shown the law to be on our side in practice as well as in theory.

For now, fear was somewhat defeated; what we had always dreaded had happened and God had proved himself greater than circumstances. It was time to replace the lies of 'the barbed wire fence' with the two truths that 'To be a Turk can also mean to be a Christian' and 'To be a Christian Turk is not only legal but legitimate'. This would be a protective wall to the Turkish church. Like the wall built by Nehemiah, it should have clear gates of entry so those seeking the fountain of life might more easily find him.

10

Follow the Son

If winters can be cold in Ankara, summers are long, hot and dry. Although we were glad to be without the draining humidity of the coastal cities, we often longed for a sea breeze. The occasional thunderstorm which cooled everything down was very welcome. It amazed us that in a few minutes a heavy downpour could turn our road into a river. Passers-by would remove their shoes and paddle for a while, yet within half an hour all could be dry again.

During the hottest months rich families would move to their summer houses by the sea, leaving their men folk to work in the city and commute at weekends. Poorer families would return to relatives back in the villages living off the land, and work in the fields.

For the Christians in Ankara, a summer high-light was the annual believers' camp. These two-week events had been started in the 1960s by Christian workers. A site, usually in an olive grove, was rented on the coast of the Marmara Sea near Bursa. Tents were pitched and though conditions were basic, the fellowship became richer as the years passed and the church grew.

Those running the camps now were from minority Christian backgrounds in Istanbul. They were amongst the finest believers in the country. Not only did they work hard and serve tirelessly but, even more important, they loved Muslims and readily accepted new converts as brothers.

Unfortunately, this was not always true of other members of the traditional Christian communities in Istanbul: the Armenians, Greeks and Assyrians. As a result of long centuries under oppressive Ottoman Turkish rule they had become locked into a defensive, ghetto mentality. When a new Turkish believer appeared they were often fearful he might be an informer and were suspicious of his motives. Quite a few believed that it was impossible for a Muslim to really become a Christian! As a result, the new Turkish believers often sensed the suspicion and, feeling rejected, quietly slipped away. However, there were beautiful exceptions and the camp was a good opportunity to experience and express unity.

For me, the camp was always better in retrospect, as it was never without incident. On one occasion our car died en route and had to be surrendered to Customs, because it had foreign number plates. I had taken far too much luggage and still remember the embarrassment of arriving by tractor, with what seemed like all our worldly goods filling the trailer. I also recall attacks by stinging bees, a scorpion in the tent, huge moths that came out of the trees at dusk, cut feet from sharp mussels, children with diarrhoea and swollen taste buds, which made eating most difficult. Once we were totally washed out by five hours of freak rain and then there was the time strong winds threatened to blow the tents away completely!

Despite all these difficulties, we always said we had a great time. Maybe it was something to do with worshipping together in the cool evenings in an olive grove, overlooking a moonlit sea. Perhaps like Abraham, coming out of our tent and looking up to the stars, our eyes were lifted to a big God for whom nothing was impossible. It was at summer camp that Christians of all ages from Turkey gathered to be church to one another and express worship to God together on truly Turkish soil.

The drive from Ankara to the Bursa camp took us past field after field of sunflowers. It was a breathtaking sight – row upon row of uplifted yellow heads all looking to the sun for light and life and, as their name suggests, looking like the sun, too. In the same way the Christians in Turkey seeking to be like Christ were looking to the Son for the next move.

Many believers felt that if the legitimacy of Christianity was to be established, the time had come to try to change their Identity Cards. In Turkey everyone is required to carry this form of identification. The individual's photograph is accompanied by personal details including religion. Since there was a procedure whereby a nominal Christian could become Muslim, then the reverse should also be possible. In Ankara no one wanted to be the first to go round various government offices and risk verbal abuse from conservative civil servants. In the end a couple who were expecting their first baby found the courage. They didn't want their child to have 'Muslim' automatically written on her card. When their daughter was born, they named her 'Sevgi' which means 'love'. In a very real and practical way, love cast out fear and Sevgi opened the way for others to follow.

Sir Fred Catherwood, an evangelical Christian and then vice-president of the European parliament, had visited Ankara, discussed Protestant rights to worship with government ministers, and set up a meeting for three Turkish church leaders with the Director of Religious Affairs. It was made clear that religious gatherings must take place in buildings designated for that purpose like a mosque or a church. As there were no suitable buildings for the Protestant congregations springing up in Turkey, their need to rent, buy or build property was recognised and their freedom to do so affirmed. Of course, the places of Protestant Christian worship would have to be publicly declared to the local authorities and the changing of ID cards was seen by the believers as a prerequisite step.

The correspondence course had always been an important filter or entry gate for interested people. In fact half of all the believers in Turkey had found the Lord through contact with the course. In the 1960s, when it began, coupons advertising the course would be posted from abroad or distributed by short-term teams, so as not to incriminate long-term workers or nationals. The address was in Europe and when inquiries came they were forwarded to the workers in Turkey. A foreign address led to some interesting responses:

'Can you send me 10,000 Swiss francs?'

'Can you send me a visa for your country?'

'Can you send me a wife?'

In the early 1980s, Dave, the leader of the coursework in Turkey, was convinced that a local address would greatly improve the quality of response. After all, he argued, with Turkey's secular constitution guaranteeing religious freedom, such a course should be legal!

With that step of faith came a rise in quality and quantity of response. Dave, who had married Pam, our friend from Ankara, and their course team in Istanbul were now looking to the

Lord for more. They found a national newspaper that was willing to publish advertisements. Responses surged to an all-time high and from their tiny office the team dealt with the inquiries, mailing Scriptures, courses and helpful books while also arranging visits to committed seekers.

The growth of the work was not without harassment, especially for Dave. Pam, too, who suffered from claustrophobia, found herself confined in dreadfully cramped Turkish police cells more than once! Slowly, however, the course ministry was involving workers from various cities and mission agencies in visiting and the follow-up of course students. As it developed, some local believers began to catch the vision.

From the responses it was clear that there were opportunities for church-planting teams in some of the smaller cities. Looking to the Lord, it began to happen. As more new workers arrived in the major cities, God began to call individuals, couples, families who already had a knowledge of the language and culture to form teams to pioneer new situations. Two mature Irish sisters felt God was leading them to a city in the south-east of the country. No one wanted them to go alone and we prayed for others to be called. Just at that time we read the exploits of Mildred Cable who, together with her friends Francesca and Evangeline French, travelled in Central Asia in the nineteenth century. We felt we dare not hinder these godly women. However, at the eleventh hour, a Mennonite family decided to join them.

God had heard our prayers and was sending many more labourers into his harvest field. We didn't all know each other as we had done when we first arrived. The face of mission worldwide was changing. It was no longer a North American/European prerogative. South Koreans had already arrived and were growing in numbers. The Latin Americans with their warmth in relationships and fiery witness were coming too. Now with the abolition of apartheid, the strong, dedicated South Africans were welcome abroad and were being released into mission.

We had to learn how to work together. Not only that, we had to remember our role as servants and encourage national leadership. Meetings at regular intervals were established for leaders, both foreign and Turkish, to help facilitate communication and maintain unity. As we looked to God, we knew he wanted us to be big-hearted towards each other, just as the Lord was towards us.

Sunflowers have very large centres, bulging with seeds. It's great fun to nibble them with a group of friends. Street sellers wander through parks and tea gardens shouting, 'Enjoyment, enjoyment' as they set up their portable stalls and pour seeds into funnels of newsprint to be bought for a few Turkish liras. I remember telling one such youth that Emma, who was small at the time, didn't know how to eat them. 'Oh!' he exclaimed in disbelief, 'Don't you have any "enjoyment" in your country?'

Yes, we needed a sense of fun and enjoyment, to be able to laugh at ourselves and realise our own blind spots when confronted with the views of others.

In Ankara we learned to work with friends so different from ourselves culturally and, also, theologically. For some years Julyan jointly led the fellowship with Steve, the leader of a conservative American mission, and Hanwoo, a Korean of the Yonghi Cho variety. It was truly enriching! We found as we submitted to one another that, when faced with a specific situation, there could be a changing of minds as love led us through.

Of course, the seeds also represented the word of God. Ian, from Canada, was eager to see the New Testament, now available in modern Turkish, more widely distributed. It had become an invaluable resource to the Christians, yet its evangelistic potential remained largely untapped as outlets were so few. Secular bookshops were hesitant to stock it but, after much prayer, Ian discovered that the pavement sellers were willing to buy it from him cheaply. Soon, every secondhand bookstall in downtown Ankara had its pile of red *Mujde*, which means 'Good News'. It wasn't long before the regular bookshops, noting the speedy turnover, lowered their resistance and began to stock the New Testament too.

Sunflowers ultimately are farmed neither for their beauty nor their fun. The seeds are crushed for their oil which is then exported far and near. The oil is valuable to the farmer. In the same way the oil of the Holy Spirit flowing from a crushed heart is precious to God.

Harriet, who had been a nursery teacher in Holland, had arrived with a burden for the children of Turkey. She was a great inspiration, helping to establish a good Sunday School in Ankara and to develop suitable materials for it. Children gravitated to her and her German flatmate. Soon they were having parties for neighbourhood children.

The situation was very delicate. Turkish law prohibits the proselytising of minors yet God was clearly leading these women. With lots of prayer coverage and gifts of wisdom they were able to share sensitively with the parents, and also teach these neighbourhood children many precious truths about God. Harriet married John, and her desire to reach the children of Turkey grew stronger.

A neighbour's child was attending a class at a school for children with special needs. Those with severe learning difficulties are thought of as shameful in Turkey and little or no stimulation is given. The teacher heard of Harriet's interest and invited her to visit the school one Monday morning. Harriet was excited about the prospect of being with these children, the ones considered unlovely, and being able to bless them in the name of Jesus.

The weekend before the proposed school visit, John and Harriet set out for Greece early on Friday, in order to renew their visas and be back in time for Harriet's visit to the special needs class. Since the arrests the previous year, John, like Julyan, had lost his residence permit. In order to stay in the country he was required to exit every three months, spend the night across the border and return the next day with a new tourist visa. Unknown to us an accident half-way to Istanbul had resulted in their car being written off, leaving John with a punctured liver and Harriet with a shattered jaw.

No one knew that anything was wrong until John phoned us. They had been brought back to Ankara by ambulance. John was to be discharged but Harriet was to stay longer in hospital. I made my way there as soon as I could, not knowing what to expect. She had been doing so well with relationships and the language, and new opportunities were opening up. Why had God let this happen?

Around the bed there were so many visitors, I could hardly get near her – Turkish believers,

neighbours, Iranian refugee friends and foreigners like myself. Her mouth and jaw seemed
full of wires, and she could only speak with dif-
ficulty. The greatest pain was in her hand and
we later discovered some glass had been
stitched inside. As I looked at her face, it was as
if Satan had slapped it in an attempt to shut her
up for daring to tell little ones of God's love.

I couldn't think of anything helpful to say but
as I squeezed nearer she turned to me and
through almost closed teeth she managed:

'I'm praising the Lord.'

Tears welled up in my eyes. No! I didn't have
to somehow defend God in the situation. He
was still with her and my attention was drawn
to the name card above her bed. A mistake had
been made in the spelling of her surname.
Instead of 'Harriet Cornelius' was written 'Harriet Holiness'. Yes, that was the oil. A big
setback to a vision, a disappointed heart yet one
that was praising and trusting still.

And how the vision grew and is still growing.
Many said it was impossible but Harriet pioneered annual camps for Christian children and
friends from around the country – children
having a chance to grow up following Jesus,
becoming more like him in character. A bi-
monthly magazine helped them to learn more
and keep in touch with each other for encouragement and support. There were seminars to
teach Turkish believers how to work with

children. A company was formed and a project begun – the writing of a children's Bible with pictures.

Harriet's heart used to ache when she passed the orphanage. Despite the well- equipped play area outside, the children always seemed to be indoors. Sadly the staff were overworked and underpaid, without the motivation for change. Regular visits there began a relationship, that led to Harriet and some friends being given a room and a group of children with severe learning difficulties, to work with as they pleased. God didn't forget her desire to love the unlovely and show what his love could do.

God was certainly expanding his work in Turkey, sending more labourers and raising up new ministries. None of it was without sacrifice but as the momentum grew, the blessing of being co-workers with God greatly outweighed any cost. Like the sunflowers we were learning to follow the Son!

As we were driving to that first summer camp so many years before, we learned a lot from the sunflowers. We noticed how faithfully their bright yellow faces turned responsively to the moving of the sun. By the middle of the afternoon, however, the sun was no longer high in the sky. Though still visible, it was not shining down on us as strongly as before. To our dismay the fields of sunflowers were no longer looking to a fading glory. They had all turned around facing the other direction. Their heads were down and then we realised they were ready for a new day to dawn.

It was important to recognise when the Lord was no longer leading in a direction and be willing to stop, and wait for vision and the next piece of the plan. Julyan and I knew that as the children got older there would be big decisions ahead. We wanted to have responsive hearts, so that our remaining years might be as productive for God as possible.

That summer of 1989 we had a wedding in Turkey. Our good friend Ayshe was greatly respected by the Christian young men in Ankara. They appreciated her wise counsel and would often ask her for advice but there was no one suitable as a husband for her. Everyone was delighted when Hasan, a wonderful Christian dentist from Izmir, proposed. Shortly after their marriage they went east where Hasan would complete his military service. It was such a special day and such a beautiful bride. In Turkish style she wore a red ribbon around the waist of her white wedding gown while the groom wore a matching red arm band to signify purity. It seemed fitting as this was a marriage truly bought by the pure blood of Jesus.

The Turkish bride of Christ, however, was far from ready. There were many in Turkey and also in the even more unreachable Turkic States of the Soviet Union, who had never heard the

gospel. Yet we know that one day Christ's bride,
gathered from every people, tribe and nation,
will be complete. Like a beautiful field of sunflowers, all facing him together and longing for
his coming she will cry, 'Come Lord Jesus', and
he will surely come.

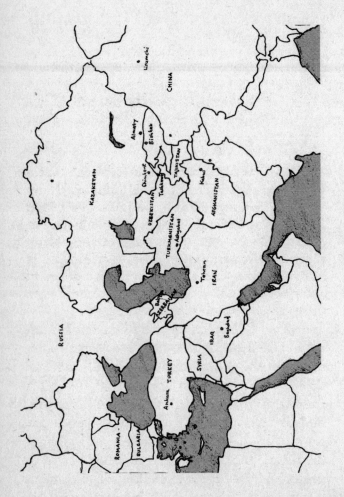

The Turkic World

11

To Russia with Love

To the world's amazement, in 1989 the Berlin Wall came down. The Soviet Union opened up and reaching the Turkic peoples of Central Asia was at last a possibility. Julyan began to plan a trip to Soviet Azerbaijan with Ferhat, an Azeri believer from Iran. The Azeri people of northern Iran and those over the border in Azerbaijan speak a Turkish dialect similar to the Turkish spoken in modern Turkey.

Ferhat and his family had fled from Tehran when his Christian activities had come to the notice of the police, and, as a result, he was under threat of imprisonment there. As a translator and writer of Christian literature, he was anxious to see if materials produced for Iranian Azeris could also be used amongst the people of Azerbaijan. Ferhat had begun to pastor what had become a fellowship of Iranian refugees in Ankara. With his big heart for

God, he and his family were a blessing to all the believers and Christian workers in the city.

Since the troubled year of 1988 and the resultant loss of our residence permit, I had schooled Emma at home. For a while we had expected to be deported but when we realised we could continue in Turkey on tourist visas, we preferred not to draw attention to our situation by attempting to register at school. Samim was also school age now, and a group of mums got together to begin a one-roomed school in the basement of the building next door to ours. As I was a primary school teacher, I taught the basics in the mornings and other parents took turns to help with special lessons in the afternoons. There were just seven children, including Ferhat's son Stephen. Despite his limited English, Stephen was the life and soul of the class.

Julyan was eager to travel to Azerbaijan to discover the needs and the opportunities for ministry there. When Ferhat was unable to get a visa, he began to wonder about another travelling companion. That night we watched a video about a family whose adventure included a shipwreck and an attack by a large bear. The decision was unanimous. We, too, would have a family adventure and go to Russia with love!

Early one afternoon just before Christmas 1990, we set out on our sixteen-hour bus trip along the Black Sea coast to the border with Georgia. We arrived very early and waited until mid-morning for the custom officials to begin their work for the day. It was a fresh December morning and the border guards with their long coats, high boots and furry hats looked so, so Russian. Any feelings of apprehension were quickly relieved by Jilda, their spaniel, whose friendly antics produced squeals of delight from Emma and Samim.

While we waited, we talked with some Azeri Turks who were returning from a shopping spree in Trabzon. Our language practice taught us the various word changes necessary to communicate well and we were also encouraged by their positive reaction to Azeri gospel literature.

From this time on we were longing to reach Baku, our target city, but getting there proved harder than we had anticipated. We had been scheduled to stay the night in Batumi, flying on to Baku via Tbilisi the next day.

Our first impressions of Russia came from this seaside border town in Georgia. Our hotel was big and dirty with mould growing on the walls. The curtain rails were either broken or missing many hooks. The atmosphere was depressing. There seemed to be shortages of everything except alcohol! Julyan woke in the night with asthma and witnessed the drunken antics of a party of Poles.

In the morning we walked in a nearby park and were surprised to see so many stray dogs. One with distinctive markings was limping with what looked like a broken paw. Instinctively, I prayed and later that day we met what seemed to be the same dog walking quite normally. Personally, I took it as a great encouragement to pray for the broken people of Russia.

We flew on to Tbilisi, the capital of Georgia, and were told to return in the evening to fly on to Baku. I drew a church for the taxi driver and he drove us to a large Orthodox building in the city centre. With the resurgence of nationalism, Georgia was remembering her Christian roots. The church was filled with people of all ages kissing the icons and lighting candles. Sadly, we couldn't see a Bible anywhere.

Soon we found ourselves making friends with a young priest in training and being invited across the road to the seminary for lunch. I felt quite conspicuous being the only woman in sight, but everyone was friendly, enjoying the opportunity to practise their English.

The dining room consisted of long trestle tables and benches where we sat supping borsch with a group of English-speakers. They were fascinated by our mission – a British family working with a church in Turkey. The concept of reaching Muslims was obviously foreign to them and as Julyan showed them verses from the Bible such as Matthew 28:19–20 they looked on in disbelief as if they had never read them before.

We spent the afternoon in a dingy tea house with Bagrat, the student priest who had become our friend. The tea was poured into big glasses from a large floral teapot. By now Samim was wearing a Georgian hat and the children amused themselves crunching the indissoluble sugar lumps. Russians put them between their teeth and drink the tea through them.

Transport back to the airport seemed impossible until our new friend persuaded the police to take us! The bad news was that there would be no available seats in the little plane to Baku for several days. Not being fond of flying I was quite happy to take the overnight train.

However, the train was very old and very slow. The windows were so dirty it was hard to see out. During the night we heard a crashing noise in the corridor and found a window had blown in. It was another sixteen-hour journey for which we hadn't taken enough food or drink. There was nothing to eat on the train and, unlike Turkey, there were no food sellers on the platforms as we stopped at stations along the way.

In the morning we befriended an Azeri young man and his Jewish wife. They generously shared their cup of lemon tea with us.

Again there was no transport from the station
and they walked with us to our hotel.

At last we could communicate freely and
with only two days left we cried to God to pack
it with his agenda. Everyone we met was
thrilled to speak Turkish with us. The hotel
nicknamed us *bizimkiler* which means 'our
people'. They were not at all impressed by our
Britishness, but by the fact that we had come
from the 'homeland' – Turkey.

We had one contact in Baku, an Azeri
believer called Lachin and that evening we had
a great time exchanging testimonies. He told us
how he had cried out to God to save him when
the brakes of the bus he was driving failed.
When the bus came to a halt at the bottom of the
hill, he knew God had answered his prayer.
Shortly afterwards he met Christians who led
him to Christ.

There were few Christian Azeris in Baku –
two or three meeting with the Seventh Day
Adventists, a few with the Pentecostals and
Lachin with the Baptists. Saturday was spent
with the Adventists where we met a delightful
family who welcomed us to their home.
Sevinch, their daughter, who studied music at
the Conservatory, spoke and sang for the tape
we made and checked some translation work
for our Iranian friend in Ankara. Emma and
Samim enjoyed the food and played with
granddaughter Fogia.

Our day with the Baptist church on Sunday was very special. Everyone there was Russian apart from Lachin and two girls who had Russian mothers but Azeri fathers who were Muslim. We found it sad that although they had lived all their lives in Azerbaijan they had never learnt their fathers' language.

Communication with the elders before the meeting was done through Lachin who spoke both Russian and Azeri. Later we met an Ethiopian student in the congregation who spoke English and he helped me when I talked with the Russian ladies over lunch.

The meeting began. Julyan was on the platform with pastor Nicolai and Lachin. I was at one side with the children. The first hymn brought tears to my eyes: beautiful Russian singing in the minor key. I looked out over the congregation – rows and rows of sixty-year-old women in ethnic-style headscarves. Tears flowed freely from my eyes. They had sung so faithfully through the years of atheistic Communism. Did they realise their preciousness to God? Had they any idea how much the world-wide church had prayed for them? Did they know how much we loved them? If I looked again I would move into noisy sobbing. I stared straight ahead to the choir – rows of pretty girls in modest Western dress; but where were the young men for them to marry? There were none! I glanced up at the platform. Julyan, with wet eyes, had a serious prayerful gaze. Pastor Nicolai, a godly man, looked weary. Then my eyes fell on Lachin. Azeri Lachin, grinning from ear to ear, was feverishly translating from Russian into his mother tongue for his new-found brother in the Lord. What joy!

The service lasted for two and a half hours with much singing by the congregation and the choir. There were prayers, three messages including one from Julyan, and a time of private prayer during which some prayed silently, some audibly. Emma and Samim aged ten and seven must have been quite moved by the atmosphere as their behaviour throughout was impeccable.

Julyan brought greetings from the Turkish church and our own home churches in Glasgow and Manchester. The congregation immediately stood up to receive them and sat down again. A surprised Julyan continued to talk enthusiastically about what God was doing in these days in the Muslim world. There were gasps and shining eyes as many began to see the implications for themselves.

Afterwards the elders had many questions. They talked of their need of materials in the Azeri language. Could Turkish believers come and help in their evangelistic efforts? They would hire a big hall. Folk would come from all over... Were we imparting a vision not only to reach the lost in Azerbaijan but also one that could unite the churches in Baku? Certainly the churches were divided. The Pentecostals had heard that we were Baptist and refused to see us. We had no time to go and argue our case!

Pastor Nicolai and the elders were imparting a vision to us, too. We would take back to Turkey a realistic missionary opportunity. Perhaps, Azerbaijan could be their Samaria.

There was more singing after lunch. They asked us to sing to them from our Turkish hymn book. We had to leave it while promising to send on a music edition. The elders gratefully received a gift sent by the Turkish church in Ankara and we agreed to keep in contact.

Svetlana made special friends with me. Her Azeri father was dead and although she knew no Turkish she warmed to our Turkishness. With the help of the Ethiopian student we shared much together. As we exchanged our addresses she asked if she could keep my pen as a memento.

Monday morning and we were off again to the airport to fly Baku – Tbilisi – Batumi. Throughout the Soviet Union the abacus is used for counting. It was fascinating to watch the clerk's fingers move so fast and so skilfully as he calculated our tickets- quite a contrast to our computerised Western airlines.

For someone who hates flying, these little planes were a nightmare. We entered from underneath, placing our luggage on a rack at the back. There was no mention of seatbelts and it felt more like being on a bus. I counted the people – thirty. I counted the life jackets – seven. Perhaps hospitality to the Turkish-speaking tourists would run out if we landed in the Caspian Sea.

Julyan, sitting further up the plane, was already sharing the gospel with yet another receptive Azeri called Kadir. Emma was lost in her book while Samim designed paper aeroplanes then pretended they were crashing – Help!

Had I ever been this fearful on a plane? In order to take my mind off myself, I turned round and began talking to the air stewardess sitting behind me. She was Georgian and did not understand me. I knew the word for church so I told her how nice the church in Tbilisi was. The young man sitting next to her got involved. He was Azeri but knew Georgian. Soon we were all conversing together and Rahiv wanted to exchange addresses in order to send me a photo of his wife and baby. He wouldn't take his pen back, insisting I keep it. Wasn't that interesting? Was it cultural? Was it just the Lord returning my pen? Certainly I wouldn't forget Svetlana or Rahiv.

Another lady I wouldn't forget was standing at the airport in Tbilisi. She stood out in the crowd with her black pigtails and her long king-fisher blue silky coat. Where did she come from? I spoke to her in Turkish and she understood me. She was from Turkmenistan where at that time there were no known believers or Turkmen Scriptures. Of course, her language sounded different and I found it hard to understand her but it was as if God were beckoning me on deeper into Central Asia.

Back in Ankara preparations began for a follow-up trip to Baku involving Turkish believers. Here was a wide open door. With their new freedom, the Azeri people had to understand that Christianity was not just for the Russians, and who better to take the message of the incarnation than Turkish Christians?

News came from Operation Mobilisation's ship *Logos II* that, while visiting Leningrad, a group of Muslims from Tajikistan had come thousands of kilometres to ask them to send a team to their country to teach them about Christ.

Yes, seventy years of atheistic Communism had left the peoples of Central Asia ignorant of all the usual Islamic arguments and very open to the gospel. How long would it last? We couldn't tell but we knew we had to move fast. Perhaps Turkey would be a good place to train people for ministry in the republics of Central Asia. Certainly, one thing was clear. We had to ask the Lord of the harvest to send more labourers for the fields were very white indeed.

12

Operation Mercy

'God doesn't love us.'

This was the cry of the Kurdish refugees as they poured over the mountains into Turkey, in the aftermath of the Gulf War of 1991. Thousands had been massacred by Iraqi soldiers, and now the survivors were forced to stay just under the snowline by Turkish soldiers, where daily there were deaths from exposure and disease.

In Turkey, the Christians felt they must do something. They had to tell the Kurds, with words and actions, that God did love them. A few ventured out east to see what could be done and came back shocked to the core. The sheer volume of human misery was in itself devastating – a hundred thousand people stuck on a mountain top without proper water or sanitation. Many were educated professionals, bewildered and ashamed of their squalor. Children, everywhere, had diarrhoea and many had

symptoms of dehydration. The camp grave-
yard already had far too many little mounds.

Early in the morning there was a call from the
UK. Two truckloads of blankets and supplies
had been donated through a Christian charity
called Global Care. Could we use them? That
very afternoon the phone rang again. This time
the call was from North Carolina, from the son
of Billy Graham…

'Franklin Graham here, from Samaritan's
Purse! What do you need? How can we help?'

'Money! We need money! Money to bring
trucks of supplies from Britain,' replied Julyan.

'You've got it,' said Franklin. 'It is on its way!'

God was clearly encouraging us to get
involved. We had the promise of supplies,
money and, of course, there were people just
longing to get out there. Ron Newby of Global
Care and George Hoffman of Samaritan's Purse
in the UK came out to see the situation for themselves. Operation Mobilisation's Middle East
area leader, Bertil, and his wife Gunnel were
with us for our annual retreat, at which we had
focused much prayer on the current crisis. Now
we all gathered together in our home to brain-
storm and decide on a plan.

We needed an umbrella organisation under
which any Christian from anywhere could
come and help. Thus Operation Mercy was
born in our lounge and Bertil, a Swedish artist,
had designed the logo within minutes. The next

morning the business cards were printed. We were now ready to send people out to pitch their tents on the mountain with the Kurds.

The thirty or so people who went and lived in the camps were now 'official' and could come and go with relative ease. They worked as servant evangelists. Servants, because they lacked professional skills but did what the secular aid groups asked them to do – digging latrines, spraying tents, picking up rubbish, washing patients in the field hospitals. Evangelists, because they kept explaining the gospel to the increasing number of Kurds and Turks who came and asked for a New Testament. With the help of Assyrian Orthodox priests, themselves refugees, they held daily children's meetings attended by up to three hundred children, with a hundred or so adults listening as well.

What the television reports didn't show, and what the Western relief agencies were unaware of, was the spiritual hunger and distress of these people.

'Why are we here, betrayed again?'

They wanted prayer for their sick and for their future and listened eagerly to stories about Jesus' love and power. Contrasting the believers' tears of compassion with the attitude of Muslim Iraqi and Turkish soldiers, some started to ponder:

'Maybe we Kurds chose the wrong religion.'

When the Kurds were sent back to Northern

Iraq, to the 'safe havens' established by the Allied forces, teams of Christian workers went with them. They manned village clinics and did social work in the camps there. The people continued to be spiritually hungry, some weeping when at last they found the New Testament for which they had longed.

In the beginning, the central administration for all this was based in our home, which meant that the telephone never stopped and the flow of people through Ankara going out east was constant. At the busiest time both Emma and Samim had chicken pox. Thankfully, they didn't feel ill, just itchy. We closed the school for a few days to allow the children to be at home and for me to man the telephone.

There were daily flights in small planes and helicopters from Diyarbakir to Zakho, the city just over the border, because of the presence out east of UN military and Western aid workers. For the first time Christian workers could live in these cities without suspicion, as foreigners were no longer an unusual phenomenon.

One of my responsibilities was to arrange flights for personnel going out with Operation Mercy. It seemed odd to be asking people their eye colour before they arrived, but Green Air, a private Turkish airline, was offering half-price tickets to ladies whose eyes were green.

Our organisation was often weak and though we did our best, we found we had to rely on

God's grace over and over again. I was trying to arrange a rendezvous for people who had never met before, in places that I had no way of visualising. Once I sent off a group of Korean doctors with a co-worker friend called Jae-hun.

'When you get to Diyarbakir airport,' I told them, 'you must find the tent of a certain British colonel. He will organise your trip by helicopter to Zakho in northern Iraq.' In my mind's eye, I imagined a colonel sitting in splendid isolation in his tent in the middle of the airport – so easy to find. Some hours later I had a phone call from Diyarbakir.

'Lenna, there is no tent here at the airport!'

'Look again,' I pleaded. 'It must be there somewhere.'

The 'somewhere', they found, was a large military airfield and camp, with hundreds of tents of military personnel, including a certain British colonel. Eventually they found him, and got their flight arranged. It seemed to me that God's grace was like a massive safety pin that somehow pulled and held all the pieces, people and places together.

Very late one night a doctor and two older nurses arrived en route to a clinic in northern Iraq. Unfortunately, the address they had been given was incomplete and they had spent hours in a taxi trying to find us. The driver had guessed our street must be in the area around the British Embassy where foreigners usually live, while in fact we were in a completely different part of the city.

Understandably, they arrived tired and frustrated. I felt likewise! Hadn't I waited up for them when my body craved sleep! The children were still infectious and couldn't play outside or have friends in. Julyan was celebrating his fortieth birthday somewhere unreachable by phone and I was tired of it all. I felt too defensive to be sympathetic to their complaints.

Very early next morning I took them outside to the taxi rank. I was relying on the driver to take them to the airport bus that left from the railway station or *gar* as opposed to the bus station or *otogar*. As I couldn't go with them it was very important that the driver got it right.

Several times I repeated with emphasis and perhaps just a little edge,

'Please, take them to the *otogar*, not the *gar* but the *otogar*!'

Walking back into the house I felt relieved that my part was finished but then my own words echoed in my ears. Oh no, I had sent them to the bus station! I couldn't believe my foolishness.

Can you imagine what the bus station in Ankara is like? It's a place milling with people and buses going to every destination under the sun – except, of course, the airport! Drivers and bus company representatives all shout at once, competing for custom while street sellers and shoeshine boys ply their trade. Perhaps there would be a party today, with drums and dancing to send a young man off to do his military service.

How could these dear people cope without the language? They were probably still so tired and disorientated. It had been such a big decision to come. Hadn't they given of their time, their money and their skills to help the Kurds? How could I be so ungracious in my attitude towards them?

Numbly, I stood at the window looking out on the taxi rank. Would my driver come back or would he pick up another fare in town? The children were still asleep. There was nothing I could do but pray:

'Lord, be merciful to me, a sinner!'

The taxi was back. I rushed out. Flushed, I explained my mistake and asked where he had taken them. He was a big man. Already, he had a glass of tea in one hand as he leaned against his cab. With twinkling eyes he looked down at me and his free hand patted my shoulder.

'Don't worry,' he grinned. 'I knew exactly what you meant and I put them on the airport bus at the railway station.'

It was a good lesson. Often we failed but again and again as we set our hearts to be merciful, God opened the floodgates and poured down his mercy upon us. As Jesus said, 'Blessed are the merciful for they shall receive mercy.'

13

The Warm Towel

After eleven years, it wasn't easy to leave Ankara. God had been speaking to us for a while about moving on, and by the summer of 1991 we knew that the time had come.

The transition to three mid-week cell groups had released some young men into leadership and resulted in more church growth. There were other foreign Christians in the city who were giving them encouragement and support and several good friends had begun to suggest we move to Izmir.

Education for the children was always a consideration. The one-room school in Ankara would expand next session. New premises and a full-time teacher were planned. It was tempting to stay and yet we knew, from our schooling experience so far, that we could probably handle the children's education at home for the next two years, until Emma reached secondary level.

The fellowship in Izmir was led by a gifted brother whose father, an officer in the Turkish army, had sent him to school in England. Before starting his studies at Nottingham University, Zekai had met and visited some Christian students studying at Dundee. Through these visits and reading the New Testament, Zekai became convinced of the truth of the gospel and made his decision to follow Christ. Together with his English wife Alison, they had returned to Turkey and spent some years engineering in the eastern town of Batman before settling in Izmir with their three children.

Zekai and Alison were somewhat alone, because several key Turkish believers had left the country and some of the foreign Christians had moved. Although many came and went within the fellowship, there was a need for a strong committed core.

Thinking about relating again to a new set of people, getting involved with children's ministry, sharing in ladies' get-togethers and home Bible studies, filled me with dread. After eleven years, I still hadn't mastered all the Turkish vowel sounds and I deliberately spoke in short sentences to avoid more complicated aspects of grammar. In Ankara I was known and my stumbling Turkish accepted and understood. Here I was, however, about to begin again and I wondered how I would fit in.

The move went smoothly. We found a nice

clean first-floor flat above a shoemaker in an area where some of the believers, including Zekai and Alison, lived. Our welcome was as warm as the weather. The neighbours were friendly. As it was the end of term Emma was immediately invited upstairs to a party organised by twin boys for their classmates. There was a holiday atmosphere as we ate on our balcony and exchanged greetings with neighbours who were doing likewise. Samim was welcomed by the local boys who called for him every evening to play football in a nearby playground. Katie, the cat, was happy with her new surroundings. Though we were on the first floor, there was a convenient tree just outside Emma's bedroom balcony and the cat flap was duly fitted to the bedroom door.

Most of all we appreciated the welcome of Zekai, Alison and their family. There was a sense of knowing and being known that made us instant friends. Though the fellowship was small, it was growing and the warmth of God's presence was often felt when we gathered together. We made many good friends, both Turkish and foreign, among the Christians. In all of this I found little problem relating and I remembered a conversation I'd once had with a friend in Ankara.

I had shared with her my great struggle with language and how often I felt full to bursting and yet unable to express what was inside. Like a woman with an engorged breast, I was full of milk yet it was coming so slowly and painfully, drop by drop.

Norita, whose Turkish was excellent and who was also an experienced mother, reminded me, 'You must keep feeding, hard though it is, until eventually the flow comes.'

Of course, I knew she was right and yet it seemed too painful. When something is hard and difficult, that's the last thing I want to do. 'I can't' often becomes 'I won't'. To try and fail, with the accompanying sense of embarrassment and humiliation, is too much to bear.

Now, here in Izmir, I remembered something else that can be done. While feeding is continued a warm towel is applied. Oh, how it relieves the hardness and discomfort in the breast, allowing the milk to flow freely.

Izmir had become like a warm towel to me. The warmth of friendship and fellowship in the Holy Spirit allowed me to relax and be myself at a deeper level with God. Just as Jesus wrapped a towel around his waist and washed the disciples' feet, he was willing to give his towel to me. There was no sense of worthlessness coming with the towel but a true humility from the Holy Spirit as I enjoyed deeper freedom in Christ to be a child of God.

It was fun to see God use my natural love of animals to develop different relationships in Izmir. Erol was a retired Turkish gentleman who lived upstairs. We fed cats on the pavement together in the evenings and had many a spiritual conversation as the strays rubbed against our legs.

When the local estate agent took a heart attack and died in the street we teamed up again. The body had to lie covered in newspaper until the situation was checked by the Public Prosecutor. A crowd of relatives and friends gathered and had to wait several hours by the roadside. Erol agreed to help me take tea to them all. Being used to preparing large quantities of tea for the Ankara church, it was a small thing to serve these sad mourners. However, it drew great attention in the neighbourhood and for days the foreigner's 'good deed' was discussed.

Yahya, the shoemaker underneath, even counted how many glasses I made and was very impressed. He already knew some of the Christians and was showing interest.

One morning a pigeon flew onto the balcony. It seemed unwell and by afternoon it had died. As I carried it downstairs to the dustbin, Yahya came out of his shop and gently examined the still-warm bird. Yes, it was quite dead and for just a moment we shared a little sadness together. After disposing of it he smiled from the shop doorway and beckoned me to follow. I'd been inside before but I had never noticed the old curtain that hung across the back wall.

He drew it to one side and there was an ancient bathtub and three beautiful, spotless white doves on a perch. I felt very privileged as if I'd peeked into the pride of his life or entered his holy of holies.

Oh, that he would know his preciousness to the God of all creation and understand that the Father without whose knowledge no bird falls to the ground had counted the very hairs on his head.

Yahya began studying the Bible with Randy, another Christian worker. So often in Turkey we saw the evangelism concept of one planting , one watering and God giving the growth. As we worked together to draw people to Jesus our fellowship was rich. Our deepest longing was to see God do more in our midst. It was 'God's' work not 'my' work, making it easier to rejoice and weep with one another.

Perhaps our biggest animal adventure in Izmir was with a dog. It was early summer and each morning we had 'home school' on the balcony. For at least two weeks we kept noticing a stray mongrel pass by our building. From her blood-covered neck hung a large stone. We so wanted to untie the string but she was much too afraid to come near. It became a little family prayer project and one Sunday we arrived home to find her lying on our doorstep.

We cut off the 'stone' but realised the string was embedded in her neck and quite impossible to remove. She followed us upstairs onto the balcony and we phoned the Animal Protection League. The president of this group was a large lady called Semra who arrived with two young vets. Soon an operation was being performed and the string removed. It turned out to be a tiny piece of nylon rope that had been tied around when the dog was a puppy. As she grew it had worked its way further and further into her neck. The 'stone' on examination proved to be solid blood that had dripped onto the knot under her chin.

All three were amazed at her trust and they named her 'Guven' which means just that. Seemingly, Semra had had many calls reporting this dog as a health hazard and she had been trying to catch her for weeks. It was good to be able to testify to answered prayer in Jesus' name and she pronounced with great drama in broken English, 'This is the God!'

Sadly, after recuperation Guven went back to the streets. We had arranged for her to go to live on a farm but we could never persuade her to climb into the car.

Our adventure with Guven was similar to our experiences with some of the believers. There seemed to be deep emotional hurts, dating back to childhood, which weighed them down spiritually. We longed for breakthroughs, and yet it was so hard to get near the painful areas. Wounded people would sometimes flee from the Lord and the source of help instead of to him, keeping themselves on the fringe with stunted spiritual growth.

Unconfessed sin also kept people from growing spiritually. Fatma was part gypsy and had many relatives in an old area of town around the castle. The houses were built into the hillside like rabbit warrens. Once a week Fatma and I would visit Ballikuyu or the 'honey well' together and there would always be opportunities to tell a story of Jesus or pray for the sick and the troubled.

One evening many gathered in a little house to watch the Jesus film. It was so thrilling to witness the response. There were gasps of delight as Jesus performed miracles of compassion for marginalised people, such as themselves, and there was a shaking of fists at the Pharisees as they came against the hero of the film. The tea house owner asked if he could keep the video to show to his customers and, of course, we obliged him with a copy.

Our relationship with Fatma came to a sad end. She had told us she was a widow and many times we'd heard the story of her husband's tragic death. One night, however, news came that she was in hospital, having been stabbed many times by her estranged husband. She had gone to his kebab stand to ask for money, and he had attacked her with his bread knife. The fellowship rallied to help, feeling pity more than anything else. She survived the ordeal, but when more lies about her personal life came to light, including an affair with a man she had introduced to us all as her brother, she was unable to let go and come clean.

Despite the pastoral disappointments the core group was growing. God was working, bringing more people to himself with baptisms and great rejoicing. Baptisms in Turkey were always a source of huge encouragement to everyone. Sometimes they took place in the sea at the annual summer camp but usually fellowships liked to organise them locally. In Ankara we had no baptistry facilities and whenever possible, we went outside the city to the nearest river or lake and had a big picnic. Our joyful celebration was infectious and brought us naturally into conversations with other picnickers, making the event a true act of witness. There was always an abundance of homemade food and Turkish tea, which we shared with everyone around.

In the summer months we could always rely on good weather but sometimes that caused its own difficulties. Once, the river we planned to use had dried up to little more than a muddy stream, and immersing Orhan who was very tall was not easy.

When we all drove out to a lake with Elif, she kept telling us about her hatred of frogs and how she was sure that she would emerge from her baptism with one on her head! However, our problem was not frogs after all. When we arrived we found a herd of cows standing in the water because of the heat. Undaunted, Elif was baptised and gave testimony to the grace she had found in Christ.

One of the most moving baptisms I witnessed in Ankara was that of Serdar. He had become interested in Christianity while working as a tour guide in Cappadocia. The frescoes in the catacombs intrigued him and in order to improve his knowledge he bought a New Testament. A crime he had committed prior to becoming a Christian caught up with him and he asked if he could be baptised before beginning his prison sentence. That Sunday he was baptised in our bathtub. Our bathroom was small but as many of us as possible crammed in to watch.

Now, in Izmir, there was a lovely location for our baptismal picnics. An American family linked to the fellowship had a rambling garden that was part olive grove. There, in the shade of a large fig tree was an olive press, a cylindrical concrete construction about a metre high and two metres in diameter. When it was filled with water it became a small pool, perfect for our purposes.

As the work grew in Izmir, the flat used as a meeting place was often packed, with lots of children sitting on the floor at the front. The children of the believers were a big encouragement and as I looked to the future I imagined them as strong church leaders. They were growing up with a sound concept of God and perhaps would not bring so much spiritual baggage into adult life. There was an eagerness to learn God's word and their prayers were often a challenge to my faith.

The correspondence course continued to bring growth, and revealed responses from people in the neighbouring towns, where follow-up visits resulted in people coming to faith. At one of our picnics, Ali from Akhisar, the biblical city of Thyatira, was baptised. More and more we were seeing the importance of Izmir to the Aegean area.

On a visit to our church in Manchester we used an overhead transparency with a map of Turkey to help us to pray. At the end of the meeting, one brother said he had seen concentric rings of earthquake shock waves going out from Izmir, affecting the whole Aegean region. Imagine our surprise when we arrived back in Izmir to find there had been an earthquake measuring 5.5 on the Richter scale, centred on the bay. It had been felt throughout the surrounding provinces. We took it as an encouragement from the Lord, to work towards a strategy that sought to evangelise the Aegean area of Turkey, using Izmir as the base.

In the days of St Paul, when the Aegean area of Asia Minor was first evangelised, Ephesus had been the main city in the province and the base for the early church-planters. With a natural harbour, Ephesus was a rich and powerful trading centre. The church there, planted by Paul and nurtured by the apostle John, was so vigorous that 'the word of the Lord spread widely and grew in power' (Acts 19:20) and soon daughter churches had been planted in all the other provincial cities, including Smyrna, which was later called Izmir.

However, John's prophetic word warned the church in Ephesus not to lose her first love, or else the Lord Jesus would remove his candlestick, or his presence, from her (Revelation 2:4–6). Years later the church in Ephesus grew politically powerful and spiritually complacent. In AD 381 the Council of Ephesus honoured Mary as the 'bearer' or 'mother' of God, and perhaps the devotion of the believers began to be turned from Jesus to Mary. In any event, there were some violent earthquakes and as the harbour gradually silted up, the trade upon which the city relied moved elsewhere and people left Ephesus. The candlestick had been taken away.

In its place Smyrna became the dominant city in Asia Minor. The word to the church in Smyrna had been, 'Be faithful to the point of death, and I will give you the crown of life.' (Revelation 2:10). This was certainly fulfilled in AD 156 when the aged Polycarp, a disciple of the apostle John, was led out to be burnt alive. Given one last chance to deny his Lord he said,

'How can I blaspheme my King who saved me?' and perished in the flames.

Our desire was to see a strong church built up in Izmir, modern Smyrna, and now nicknamed 'The Pearl of the Aegean', from which believers in all the surrounding towns and villages could be supported. Isolated believers could come and find fellowship and have their feet washed. Yes, Izmir could service them and be a warm towel for the Aegean region.

Zekai had a big vision and a big heart. He felt the burden of the church like a true pastor. He also cared for the other Turkish church leaders, and encouraged them and their wives in mutual friendship, in sharing their needs and struggles together, along with their dreams and visions. He had a hunger for reality in his relationship with God and others, and a transparent lack of pretence which was so attractive in a society that gives great respect to status and position.

It was February. The whole of Europe was engulfed in snow. Much of Turkey with subzero temperatures was cold and icy. Yet in Izmir, the almond trees had blossomed! Suddenly, without warning, the first signs of spring. Just as in the vision of the almond branch given to the prophet Jeremiah, God was watching to fulfill his word (Jeremiah 1:11). He would build his church in Turkey and perhaps Izmir would be a warm towel to her, servicing and refreshing her soul.

14

They're Doing My Dance

At the outset, our stay in Izmir was to be for two years until Emma's primary schooling ended, but as time went on we kept thinking of ways to extend it. Ultimately, however, the clash between local church involvement and directing part of an international organisation became acute. With teams living in eight cities, a Kurdish work over the border and a training ministry for Central Asia, Julyan was travelling more and more.

In July 1993 we moved to Istanbul and the centre of Christian work for the Turkic world. We already knew many of the Christian workers and Turkish believers and for the children there was a suitable school – Martyn International Academy. It was named after the English missionary scholar Henry Martyn, whose heart for Muslims led him to translate the New Testament into Arabic and Persian, and who died in Turkey in 1812. I agreed to teach the beginners' class two days each week and our involvement there proved to be a blessing for us all.

Although we felt the necessity of the move, initially only Katie, the cat, was truly excited by it. Our new house was on the ground floor with the living room to the back opening out into its very own 'secret' garden! It was delightfully overgrown with a wild bank of lavender hydrangeas, a tiny plum tree, a vine and enormous pink hollyhocks that peeped in the windows. On holiday by the Black Sea we met a large tortoise called Kumbaba, who agreed to come home with us and make our garden complete.

The children warmed to the move as they made friends. The neighbours were fine people and Emma and Melis, who lived next door, were soon spending hours together sitting in the doorway chatting. Samim was happy to be at last living in the home city of his favourite football team. Istanbul sports three teams and almost everyone in the country supports one of them. Ours was Beshiktash and sharing this important information with our new landlord sealed our friendship, as he and his family were also fans of the 'Black Eagles'.

In Istanbul we began attending an international fellowship which had been formed to meet the spiritual needs of the foreign Christian workers on the Asian side of the city. The traditional, conservative, evangelical style of worship seemed flat after the excitement of pioneering new churches of Muslim converts.

Shortly after our arrival in Istanbul, the children and I were smitten with head lice which proved to be immune to the chemist's preparations and all the home remedies suggested by friends. Day by day the problem got worse instead of better. This particularly virulent strain of creepy-crawly seemed invincible! One night, following the advice of a 'friend', I applied lotion for body lice to my head. Donning a plastic bag to protect the pillow case, I went to bed. Julyan, who had remained completely unaffected by this infestation, was dropping off to sleep nicely beside me. As I lay there, with plastic rustling in my ears and monsters wrestling in my hair, I began to feel nauseated.

'I'm feeling sick!' I moaned.

Julyan's sleepy voice replied, 'Your scalp is probably absorbing poison from the lotion!'

I leapt out of bed, staggered to the bathroom and spent the next hour or so showering my head. In the morning the lice were all alive and apparently thriving! After ten days of near quarantine, Harriet, our friend from Ankara sent a Dutch preparation up to us by bus, and it cleared the problem at once. By this time I was so desperate for fellowship, that I emerged from isolation eager to embrace my new life in Istanbul.

Actually, it was impossible not to fall in love with a city so steeped in history. There was so much to see: the Sultan's palaces, Byzantine mosaics, monuments, museums, markets and mosques. One of our favourite places was Florence Nightingale's hospital at the barracks in Scutari, now known as Uskudar. Our house was on the Asian side of the city but frequently we crossed by 'sea bus', a kind of high speed ferry, or took a bus over the Bosphoros bridge to Europe!

Despite our growing love for the city, it was not such an easy place to live, with horrific traffic congestion and a grossly insufficient water supply for the population of over ten million. Droughts and leaks in the old pipelines resulted in some areas having water for limited hours a day or limited days a week.

In Ankara the dry cold winters had aggravated Julyan's eczema. Here in Istanbul dampness led to asthmatic problems, especially when mould appeared on the bedroom wall. Often, the Christian scene seemed polluted too. The work was still small, with only a few hundred Christians, yet compared to other cities in Turkey, there were many foreign workers and several churches with established local leaders and ministries.

There were regular meetings of nationals and foreigners to keep communication open and maintain unity, yet conflicts did arise. Despite being new to Istanbul, Julyan was called in several times to act as a go-between, because of his understanding of the country and the church scene.

A small Bible Institute had been established on the European side of the city. Mary had retired from many years of work amongst the Canadian Indians, and was now organising the study programme there. I had great admiration for her. Despite coming as an older woman, she had managed to learn the basics of the language. Along with her biblical knowledge and insight, Mary also had a great sense of fun that made her much loved by the Turkish believers. While Julyan taught courses in theology, I prepared and presented a short course on teaching spiritual truth to children. It was a great test for my language fluency, but my listeners were all eager to learn and participate in the lessons, making it very satisfying indeed.

Perhaps the real highlight of our stay in Istanbul was the visit of Operation Mobilisation's ship *Doulos*. The preparation for the arrival of this Christian ministry took months. Julyan and the line-up personnel made many trips to government and port officials to obtain the necessary permissions.

First it docked at Mersin, a city near biblical Tarsus and neighbouring Adana where Christian work had been especially hard over the years. We had several workers in this province of Silicea who were greatly encouraged by the events on board and the positive response of local people.

In Istanbul the book exhibition was greatly appreciated. Students who came on board were thrilled to find educational books at reasonable prices. Many had included a New Testament in their basket before arriving at the checkout.

Low-key cultural events were organised including visits for schoolchildren. Several crew members in national costume set up areas in the ship lounge, speaking and answering questions about their countries. The children would move around having their 'passports' stamped. They all loved the friendly atmosphere and the teachers were impressed by the high degree of professionalism.

Of course, the ship was a big encouragement to the Turkish Church. For many who had never been outside their own country, it was as if God's international family had come to them. There were gatherings for believers, workshops in creative arts and coffee bars in the evenings.

Some Turkish Christians worked on board as volunteers, helping in the book exhibition or working as translators. Everyone joined in with the many practical chores that make up ship life. They travelled with the *Doulos* around the Black Sea coast to Crimea, where over two hundred thousand Muslim Tatar people had recently returned to their homeland from exile in Central Asia. During the Second World War Stalin had feared they would support Hitler, so had deported them en masse to Uzbekistan. Now, because of the Soviet policy of *glasnost*, they were free to come home to Crimea and their devastated villages. The *Doulos* personnel worked with the Tatars to help rebuild their houses. It was great to have some Turkish speakers from a Muslim background who could share their faith effectively with this Turkic people group.

From the Black Sea port of Odessa, they visited the Gagauz in Moldova, the only Turkic group who are Russian Orthodox Christians, never having embraced Islam.

The Baptist churches there were experiencing revival and many Gagauz were coming to a living knowledge of Christ. These Turkic Christians were greatly challenged to meet converted Muslims. Prior to the *Doulos* visit, they had thought little of God's love and grace towards other faiths, but now many began to wonder if God had a special purpose for the Gagauz in the Turkic world. They began to pray and some determined to go to reach their fellow Turks for Christ, despite their extreme poverty.

The ship had hoped to sail on to Bulgaria but at the last minute the visit was blocked by the Orthodox Church. Meanwhile, back in Turkey, the press coverage had been so positive that the Chairman of the Izmir International Trade Fair decided he wanted the ship to come to Izmir. He bombarded the OM office in Germany with faxes promising a good berth and waiving port fees. When the planned visit to Bulgaria fell through, the *Doulos* was able to sail into Izmir instead and bring the Turkish volunteers home.

At every port an International Night was a favourite part of the ship programme. This was an evening which showcased cultural items, songs and dances in national costume from the countries represented by the Doulos staff. Local officials and dignitaries, as well as ordinary members of the public, would be invited to enjoy the colourful spectacle of, for example, the Korean Fan Dance and the Filipino Stork Dance.

Turks are themselves nationalistic and are proud of their folk dancing. Once when I was new in Ankara I was invited to an inter-university folk dance competition held in a large open-air stadium. I couldn't believe my eyes. Each university performed a well-known regional dance with appropriate costume and musical accompaniment. The performances were breathtaking and the enthusiasm of audience, cheerleaders and dancers was equal to that of any international football tournament, as scarves were waved and banners were paraded. The dances intrigued me. Some from the Black Sea region were almost Cossack in style, while others involved sequences similar to the Jewish vine step. Many of the traditional folk dances used movement to tell stories.

I watched as the dancers portrayed aspects of village life, such as working in the fields, fetching water from the well, fighting with raiders and falling in love. In my mind's eye, I looked forward to the day when a travelling Turkish dance troupe might visit the villages of Turkey communicating the story of Christ's passion in a similar manner. When the ship docked in Izmir, a Turkish folk dance group was invited to participate in the ship programme and the dancers were surely touched by the love and acceptance offered.

The International Night is always a beautiful illustration of the strong message *Doulos* brings. Yes, three hundred people from more than thirty countries can live and work together in peace when God's love makes them one. This does not make us all the same but enables us to acknowledge and enjoy our differences.

When the ship visited Istanbul we stayed on board helping with translation and cultural issues. On the Saturday afternoon, I wandered into the gymnasium and found Hazel, the Scottish schoolteacher, practising a traditional Scottish dance, the Eightsome

Reel, for the evening performance. It was such an unlikely group of people. There was an Albanian, a Swede, an American, a Dutchman, a Ghanaian, two Englishmen and one Scot. As someone raised on Scottish country dancing, I felt this was surely sacrilege but as I had been given charge of the tape recorder I obediently pressed the 'play' button.

The oh so familiar music began and a lump formed in my throat. These young people were taking it very seriously. Their footwork was good, their timing perfect, their facial expressions sincere. I, alone, was the audience and a wave of homesickness I'd hardly felt in all the years in Turkey washed over me as I said to myself:

'They're doing my dance and they're doing it for me.'

The next day was Sunday and in the afternoon there was a worship service on board for Christians in the city. The ship lounge was packed. There were Armenian and Assyrian Christians, as well as many Muslim converts from Istanbul, and some visitors from Ankara and Izmir. The church leaders and full-time workers were there from such organisations as the Bible Society. The international ship crew were represented, as were the foreign workers such as ourselves. There was so little space in the crowded room that I found myself hovering on tiptoe in a doorway, in order to see what was happening.

As the worship began, I glimpsed the sincerity of many faces and I sensed the Lord say to me:

'They're doing my dance and they're doing it for me!'

In God's eyes these hearts, united in worship, were like a beautiful dance to him. *Doulos* means 'slave' and the ship personnel had certainly worked hard, bringing so many Christians together in Istanbul. For these brief weeks the believers had been aware of being part of something global, something much bigger than themselves, and had been drawn closer to the Lord of the Dance.

For us as a family, 'the dance' went on and we left the ship to visit the teams in Central Asia who were having their retreat in Almatty, the capital of Kazakhstan. Yes, God was answering prayer and sending Christians to work in a number of the republics. Among the first to respond were Chris and Lily, our friends who had reluctantly returned to Canada from Adana some years before. Now they were in Xinjiang province on the Chinese border, reaching out to the Uighur people.

Others were working among Kazakhs, Uzbeks and Tajiks. Sadly, there were still no known believers from the Turkmen of Turkmenistan. This was not really surprising as, at that time, there were no Christian workers living there and the New Testament had only just been published that year!

The retreat gathered about thirty foreign Christian workers from a variety of nations and on the final morning we shared communion together.

'Take the cup to someone from another country and pray together', the leader suggested.

I felt the unmistakable finger of God and knew what I must do. The message of *Doulos*, still fresh in my heart, had exposed the ugly face of nationalism and I headed straight for Sue, the only Englishwoman there.

Often I'd argued that my Scottish patriotism was no more than a joke. After all, hadn't I married a Londoner? Yet, if I were honest, I knew I could never have done so, had his accent and manner not been modified by his years of living abroad.

No, we Scots stereotyped the English as arrogant and proud and there was a despising of them that seemed to be inherent to my Scottish culture. I wanted to be rid of it! I always felt defensive, as though I had to fight Scotland's battle for recognition, when in fact an inferiority complex is nothing more than inverted pride.

As we prayed together, each confessing negative attitudes from our backgrounds, I felt God bring a new lightness in my spirit.

Again, I recognised and affirmed my identity firmly in Jesus and my true citizenship in Heaven. The defensiveness gone, I felt I could dance for joy and celebrate my Scottishness all the more heartily.

15

The Stones Cry Out

The Operation Mercy team continued in Zakho, the border city of northern Iraq. They had worked with a group called 'Shelter Now' helping to facilitate the building of simple houses for the returning refugees whose own homes had been destroyed by Saddam Hussein's Iraqi army.

During that time they had got to know many Kurdish families, had improved in language and had now begun a feeding programme for malnourished babies. As the team was mostly women, this was a good ministry, allowing them to enter homes and build relationships as well as save lives.

In December of 1993 I made a brief visit. I flew from Istanbul to the city of Diyarbakir in the east of Turkey where I was met by Irma, a German girl who had made her home there. Diyarbakir, the major Kurdish city of eastern Turkey, is one of the oldest cities in the world.

The impressive black basalt stone walls had seen centuries of conflict as conqueror after conqueror broke through to capture the city. It continued to be a place of violence as Kurdish nationalists struggled for more recognition from the State and the Turkish military responded with a heavy hand.

The Kurdish language had been banned in all public places since 1924, when Kemal Ataturk wanted everyone in the modern republic of Turkey to be treated equally. He determined that all citizens of Turkey were to be Turks and refused to recognise any ethnic minorities. The official line was that the Kurds were really 'mountain Turks' who no longer spoke Turkish because they had 'forgotten their original language'. Their traditional Kurdish culture, folk songs and dances were suppressed. Even their villages were given new names of Turkish origin, replacing the old Kurdish ones. It was impossible to remove the sense of nationhood from these ten million Kurds who lived in Turkey, mostly concentrated in the east, and the dream of a homeland burned in every Kurdish heart.

This denial of their distinct identity was bitterly resented and from time to time provoked popular uprisings, which were harshly put down by the Turkish army. In 1984 the Kurdish Workers Party (the PKK), an extreme left-wing nationalist movement, launched the first of its terrorist strikes. As well as attacking Turkish soldiers, policemen, teachers and doctors, the PKK also brutally killed any Kurds who co-operated with the authorities. Tens of thousands of Turks and Kurds were killed all over eastern Turkey.

Lesley, from New Zealand, had brought Joan to see the doctor in Diyarbakir. Joan, a tall slim American woman, yellow and exhausted due to hepatitis, sat propped up in the front seat of the Land Rover. Irma and I climbed in the back.

We drove south to Mardin, a most striking and attractive town near the Syrian border. The town flows down the broad hillside near to the highway that leads to Mosul and on to Bagdad in Iraq. Stopping to eat *pide*, a kind of spicy pizza without the cheese, which we rolled up and ate with our fingers, we stretched our legs and gazed upwards to the pale sandstone buildings and the citadel on top of the hill.

This town had also known much violence and sorrow. During the First World War the Turkish government feared the Armenians of eastern Turkey would take sides with the invading Russians, and in 1915 took the decision to deport the entire population to Syria. Mardin was on the route south, and the miserable refugees spent months in temporary encampments on the plains below. Many died of disease, many died in horrific massacres at the hands of Turkish soldiers, and many were killed by Kurdish bandits on the way. Later that year the Armenians of Mardin itself, as well as the other Christian communities, the Assyrians, the Catholics and the Protestants, suffered the same fate.

The Assyrians are one of the traditional Eastern Orthodox churches, and use the old Syriac language in their liturgy. They used to be quite populous in eastern Turkey, but most have emigrated to find work in Istanbul or Europe. During the PKK uprising the few Assyrian villagers left were caught between the two sides. The PKK guerrillas would come at night demanding food and supplies at gunpoint, and then in the morning government soldiers would arrest the villagers for collaborating with the enemy.

The road was quiet with some military checkpoints. By the time we reached the town of Jizre it felt as if we had arrived at the world's end. This was such a depressed place. Bullet holes patterned the walls and many windows had been boarded up.

'Who caused the destruction?' I asked.

There were different opinions. Some said that rebel Kurds were at fault, as they would attack anyone employed and sent out by central government. Police chiefs were a prime target but even schoolteachers and doctors were not immune. Others blamed the Turkish army and military police who saw all Kurds as the enemy and would readily open fire in their zeal to combat terrorism.

Just before the border was the town of Silopi and the last chance to buy some provisions. As Lesley filled a bag with mandarin oranges, something impossible to find in Zakho, Irma chatted with the shopkeeper in the Kirmanji dialect of Kurdish. We each bought a large bottle of drinking water as there would be no running water in the house when we arrived, and no one knew when the water truck would come to fill up their tank outside.

There was no border check as we entered northern Iraq, only an enormous banner with a picture of the famous Kurdish leader, Mullah Mustafa Barzani, on a white stallion. Zakho was a sad city, much more like a large village. There were no services such as rubbish collection and waste had to be burnt regularly. We parked the Land Rover outside the whitewashed concrete house where the women working with Operation Mercy lived. They had no electricity. Usually, Lesley explained, the team would sit their solar lanterns on the flat roof by day to charge the batteries and then they could enjoy their light in the evening. This time they had forgotten.

The Kurds had suffered like the rest of Iraq from the UN sanctions imposed in 1990 after the invasion of Kuwait but, since the Kurdish rebellion, no supplies were coming up from the south at all. Saddam's soldiers had devastated Kurdistan, blowing up bridges, dynamiting houses and pouring poison down wells. They had even deliberately sown landmines in fields and orchards so that farmers could not cultivate their crops. The only food in the markets came from Turkey and was very expensive.

There was fear as the Kurds looked south. How safe were they really? Would the UN peacekeeping force remain or desert them? Many times in the past the Kurds had been deserted by the superpowers in their hour of need. Would history repeat itself? There was fear as they looked north. Some of the houses built recently by 'Shelter Now' had been bombed by the Turkish military in their frequent raids. Turkish Kurds who were members of the outlawed terrorist group, the PKK, were believed to have camps over the border in northern Iraq and the fear there of a Turkish invasion was very real.

That night we sat around the paraffin stove chatting, eating the oranges and praying by candlelight. Joan felt better, now that she could lie out flat on the couch, and she shared with us her vision to open a therapeutic feeding centre, where they could care for babies requiring hospitalisation.

The Operation Mercy team leaders were a coloured South African couple who were on furlough at the time of my visit. We had known

Julian and Peni since our days in Izmir, where working together had been such a blessing, despite the confusion of never knowing which Julian people were talking about! As we had watched them forge deep relationships with white South African Christian workers in Turkey, we saw a fine example of God's love and reconciliation power. Having known oppression most of their lives, Julian and Peni were able to empathise with the Kurds and, being coloured, they even looked like them.

Once in bed, the candle out, I expected the room to be dark but, no, the moon was shining so brightly that light streamed through the thinly woven curtain. The bedroom was icy cold. I lay under my heavy Kurdish quilt with the curtain a little open to enjoy the view. It was a beautiful sight, the moon and the stars shining over the snow-capped hills surrounding Zakho.

I couldn't sleep. I kept thinking of the stones from the walls of Diyarbakir, Mardin, Jizre, Silopi, the 'Shelter Now' houses and the hills around Zakho. How much they had witnessed of man's pride, greed and inhumanity to man. How much they cried out for justice. I thought of the shrine at Jizre, believed to be the tomb of Noah. Yes, they knew about 'the flood' and God's judgement on sin, but did the people understand the message of the rainbow and God's promise of a Saviour?

It seemed to me that the only way to silence the stones was the blood of Jesus, present and applied through the lives of his people bought to love him, sold out to praising his name. How precious to know him there, to carry his presence to fearful, hate-filled places.

The next day, Lesley remembered the solar lanterns and then we were off with Nuray, a Kurdish helper, to visit homes. They weighed and measured babies, gave out food and encouraged the families most lovingly. One baby, 'Kurdistan', who had been born in a camp and named in faith looked about six weeks old when, in fact, she was six months.

There was little work. The men stood around the market place clutching their Kalashnikov rifles with eyes full of hopelessness. Sayid, our driver, was a graduate in engineering from Mosul university and he was fortunate to have any job at all. Nuray, too, was an educated, English-speaking girl. Neither could see any future for themselves. They seemed to be broken in spirit, and I was glad that God promised to be close to such ones and that both were studying the Bible.

In every town where Christians had come there were now a few believers – the beginning of a Kurdish Church. The Operation Mercy personnel together with others had organised the translation of Luke's gospel in the Bahdanini dialect and the Jesus film had been dubbed and

shown on local TV before the electricity supply
had been cut off by Turkey.

The Christian work was humble, like the
Jesus who entered Jerusalem on a donkey.
Would the message of forgiveness be heard,
understood, received? It was the Kurds' only
hope of lasting peace. They needed reconciliation even amongst themselves. There were constant power struggles between the Patriotic
Union of Kurdistan (PUK), led by Jalal Talabani,
whose support came from the Sorani Kurdish
speakers to the south-east, and the Kurdish
Democratic Party (KDP) of Massoud Barzani,
son of Mullah Mustafa, in the north. Even
though Iraqi Kurdistan was a tiny, impover-
ished enclave struggling for its survival, these
two political parties could not avoid violent
clashes. The KDP even shelled one of the few
remaining hospitals because it was under PUK
control. Would their fighting bring even more
destruction upon the area and do their cause
more harm than good? They needed the
message of the Gospel urgently but the messengers were so few.

One of them was Sharon, or Seher, as she was
affectionately known to the Kurds. She was a
fresh-faced American girl in her early twenties.
All the nursing she knew she'd learnt in the
local hospital in Zakho. Sharon had come to
Turkey when she was just a teenager and had
been involved with the Kurds since the crisis in

1991. Most of her time was spent in the villages around the city where she would visit and often stay with local friends and their families.

Many would say she was too young and inexperienced. Certainly, she had not been through seminary and had no degree in theology or missiology. Her youth, on the other hand, had made her teachable and enabled her to learn Kurdish well. She 'belonged' to so many families with whom she would sit and share stories of Jesus. That was her passion and for that purpose God had called her.

Sharon reminded me of the baby donkey Jesus chose to take him into Jerusalem. It too was inexperienced yet chosen because the Master needed it. Jesus didn't use a big stick to beat it from behind, or a carrot out front to tempt it onwards, and yet it travelled through the noise and tumult of its day, the branches waving, the crowds shouting and the coats flung down. There was so much to distract and terrify.

Likewise for Sharon, there was no self-punishing martyr spirit that had forced her to that hard place. Nor was there a false idealism, like an unreachable carrot, leading her on. No! Jesus had called her. She felt his firm yet gentle hand upon her neck and his voice whispering encouragements in her ear. In that way she was able to carry the Lord's presence and keep going step by step in obedient trust. Perhaps that's what true faith is all about and, as Sharon served in the local hospital and spent time in the villages, she felt the breath of her creator God fill her being and say:

'I made you for this day!'

As Irma and I left on the bus from Silopi back to Diyarbakir and my flight home, the music and chatter all around us was Kurdish, but then a Turkish film began to play on the television screen. The style was similar to the British *Carry On* films with a well-known comic cast. The plot was that of a couple who were travelling our very route when they were kidnapped by the PKK!

'What if that happened to us?' I whispered somewhat nervously to Irma.

'They would respect us,' she replied quietly. 'I speak their language. It would be an enormous opportunity and we would take it.'

Yes, God had raised up living stones to witness to his truth and his love and to praise his name in all circumstances. Irma was a rock in her commitment to his cause.

As I remembered the banner of Barzani on the stallion at the entrance to Kurdistan, I thought of the picture in Revelation of Jesus, Lord of Lords and King of Kings, coming again on his white horse, and I hoped the Kurds would be ready.

16

A New White Shirt

Turks are a spiritual people. One of the delights of living and working in Turkey was the ease with which spiritual issues could be discussed. Few were real atheists. Though many young people had rejected Islam, they would find it hard to deny the reality of spiritual experience.

Formal Islam taught them about God as Creator and God as Judge. God was far away, unyielding, unknowable and yet together with all mankind they longed for closeness and reality in their spiritual life. They didn't understand that they could come to God as Father, through his Son Jesus, and know God's nearness by the presence of the Holy Spirit.

In John 14:6 Jesus explains 'I am the way and the truth and the life. No one comes to the Father except through me.' Such verses became so important as we got to know Muslims who thought of themselves as slaves of God rather than sons.

Since Islam cannot provide the assurance that comes from our confidence in God as Father, it often fails to meet deep personal needs. To cope with the crises and challenges of life, many Muslims turn to the animistic practices that were part of their cultures before the advent of Islam. In Izmir, for example, students facing exams, barren women anxious to conceive a son and mothers worried about a sick child would congregate at a certain hilltop to sacrifice chickens and pour water over the grave of a local 'saint'. This kind of behaviour, though frowned on by orthodox Islam, is very common all through the Muslim world. It is often referred to as 'folk Islam'. In Turkey these rituals are conducted by a *hoja*, a man or woman who will tell fortunes, pronounce curses or write out charms in return for a financial consideration.

When Emma was born, neighbours were eager to pin a blue bead to her clothing. These beads were supposed to ward off the 'evil eye'. Jealousy is thought of as a destructive spiritual force projected through the eye of the beholder. Something beautiful like a baby must be protected and the blue bead is believed to distract the gaze and, therefore, the evil power. Complimenting children is not appreciated as it can be interpreted as covetousness, and a positive comment must be immediately redirected to God's praise by saying *Mashalla*.

Of course, I explained our trust in God and
the security we had in knowing that the eye of
the Lord was always upon us to protect and
guide us. My words were surely tested when
Emma became very sick and I realised my trust
had to be more active. The doctor couldn't cure
her vomiting and diarrhoea, and it was only
after our church back home prayed one Sunday
morning, that the symptoms subsided.

It is common for Turks to wear charms for
protection and it was a real step of faith for
believers to give them up. Satan rules by fear
and many needed deliverance in this area.

Fierdevs was a pretty young girl who had
been given in marriage to her cousin. Other relatives were furious that she had not been given
to their son and Fierdevs began to suffer head-
aches and fainting spells. Her mother found a
piece of plastic that had been pricked many
times with a pin and pushed into a crack in the
outer wall of the house. It was the work of the
local *hoja*, who had written the curse at the
request of the jealous uncle. The smitten family
had gone from *hoja* to *hoja* in their attempt to
have it reversed but to no avail. At last, they
were advised to try 'the Christians' and they
arrived at our door.

After a short Bible study from Luke 11 on the
binding of the strong man, Julyan destroyed the
piece of paper and prayed in the powerful name
of Jesus. Fierdevs promptly 'fainted' causing us

to be somewhat alarmed until we realised she had been overcome by the Holy Spirit and 'woke' completely well.

We counselled them of their need to fill the empty house that was clean before seven spirits returned and took up residence. The family were grateful but seemed to see us as yet another *hoja* who was useful in times of crisis. Fierdevs, herself, believed in Jesus.

Turkish friends often had meaningful dreams and visions that helped them in their faith. Sometimes they would ask us to explain them. Suat began to read the New Testament. As he read the beginning of John's gospel he 'saw' Jesus and the disciples walking amongst the pages. Jesus turned and looked at Suat with eyes 'full of love and sadness'.

'Why do you think Jesus looked sad?' asked Suat. It was a joy for Julyan to explain how Jesus felt about Suat's sin and this young man gladly repented and put his faith in Christ. Another friend's father had a dream in which Abraham appeared to reassure him about his son's new faith.

In Turkey we became more aware of the importance of the supernatural, as God worked powerfully in peoples' lives. We also saw the importance of the scriptures to test, define and anchor experience in truth. Bulgaria was a good example of this as God began to move among the Turks and the gypsies there.

Through the 1980s, these people had suffered through the Communist government's campaigns to impose Bulgarian culture upon them. God in his mercy began to move, initially, through a couple of Bulgarian Pentecostal brothers reaching out with the good news. By the early 1990s there were groups meeting throughout the country. The Lord was blessing in many ways and a summer team that went to help with evangelism came back with interesting stories.

At the end of an evening meeting the Pastor had asked the team leader if he would pray for the sick to be healed.

'Oh,' said the conservative American brother, 'and how do I know it's God's will to heal?'

'Well,' said the Pastor, 'It's not so difficult. Just look out over the congregation and pray for the person next to the angel. That's the one God wants to heal now!' The Lord seemed to enjoy giving more abundantly to the poor and the rejected. For those who have not even the Word of God to guide them, he sends angels!

However, as time passed the need for scriptures and sound teaching became evident. There was confusion between healing and salvation. Some people thought that because they had been healed they must be saved, while others thought that as they hadn't been healed they couldn't be saved. In 1994 we visited the town of Plovdiv and found the groups of believers now had the Turkish New Testament which had been translated into Cyrillic script just for them. We stayed with a family who had spent some years working in Turkey, and whom God had called to Bulgaria to help with teaching and discipleship.

Kamil and Hajer were our landlords in Istanbul. They were an older retired couple for whom we had much respect. Born in the early 1930s, they had grown up in a society greatly influenced by the principles of their leader at that time – the great military general and hero of Gallipoli, Mustafa Kemal Ataturk, father of the modern Turkish nation.

In the 1920s, Ataturk had succeeded in breaking the political power of Islam. European laws were introduced and Sunday rather than Friday became the day of rest. Women were given the vote and could be elected to parliament. The Latin alphabet replaced Arabic and English became the official foreign language taught in school. Turkey had become a republic and with Ataturk's programmes of Westernisation had come a firm commitment to democracy and a secular constitution.

Kamil and Hajer thought much about God and wanted to honour him in all they did. They were Muslim but they had also been part of Ataturk's Youth Movement, and felt very uncomfortable with the rise of Islamic fundamentalism. Hajer commented once that she couldn't believe that a God who had made the flowers in such beautiful colours would want her dressed in black!

Hajer is the Turkish form of Hagar, the mother of Ishmael, whom Muslims look to as Abraham's son. Perhaps this couple represented the noblest aspirations of Turkish society – Ataturk's slogan, 'Peace at home, peace abroad', together with Hagar's sincere thirst for God.

When we visited them, we loved to talk about our families and our countries, our favourite football team and, of course, God. They would tell us about the Pillars of Islam and show us photographs of their pilgrimage to Mecca. Sometimes we were able to tell stories from the life of Jesus which were always appreciated by these friends.

The time came when we knew we should return to Scotland. After our two years in Istanbul, the school could only continue for Emma by way of correspondence course. None of us felt this was right. As well as the schooling need, there was a growing sense that in our administrative role of field leadership, we had moved from the cutting edge of hands-on ministry. We both began to hear God speak to us about Scotland in different ways. There was some work that God had for us, and reluctance gave way to expectancy as we looked forward.

Like the ancient Celts who, when embarking on a missionary journey, would climb into their small leather skin boat and let the wind lead the way, we longed to jump into our coracle and set sail.

Usually Kamil came for the rent each month but this time Hajer came too. We decided to tell them our news and Hajer was not at all surprised. While the men discussed the practical details, she explained to me that she had come specially with her husband because she was sure it was going to be an important visit. For ten nights she'd had a dream in which Julyan gave Kamil a present of a new white shirt and told him he loved him. I didn't know what to say. Immediately, I confirmed that we did indeed love them both but the white shirt required some thought.

The photographs from Mecca had shown them walking around in long white robes. Another part of the pilgrimage ritual involved the collecting of *Zamzam* water. This was considered very special water as it was drawn from the well God opened for Hagar and Ishmael in the desert. (Mohammed associates it with Mecca though we know geographically it was in the Negev). Enough water had to be brought back to share the blessing with all the relatives.

Surely, the new white shirt was Jesus, himself, not a reward for good works but the pure gift of God. He would be to them garments of salvation, robes of righteousness, wedding clothes for the great banquet, not in Mecca but in Heaven itself! And just as God had opened Hagar's eyes to see the well in the desert, couldn't he open their eyes to see Jesus, the living water springing up to eternal life?

Wasn't that God's desire for all the descendants of Ishmael, the offspring of Abraham whom he had promised to bless for Abraham's sake? (Genesis 17:20)

Postscript – Table in the Wilderness

Our last months in Turkey were full of farewells. We celebrated Easter with our Izmir friends. The children presented a most moving passion play and the newly bought church building was already full to capacity. It was a great encouragement also to visit the Bible Society bookshop that had just opened near the centre of town.

A weekend retreat in Iskenderun in a lovely old monastery enabled us to say goodbye to all the workers in the south-east of the country. Our sisters from Northern Ireland were there and we shared a final supper with them, after everyone else had gone to bed. Our bus back to Istanbul was at some unearthly time the next morning. We rose when it was still dark and tiptoed to the kitchen to make ourselves a drink. To our surprise we found Irma and an early breakfast waiting for us. Yes! we were leaving a very special family behind.

Several Ankara friends came to visit us during our final months in Istanbul 'to pay their last respects'. One warm evening we sat outside with Ozjan, a mature drama student who had become very involved in the children's camps. As we ate our water melon he told me that a group of them in Ankara had been reminiscing together and had talked about me. I wondered what they had said. It was obviously positive as he was smiling. Had they remembered my prayers, my faith, my wisdom or perhaps my words of encouragement? No! none of these!

'You always kept our tea glasses full,' he continued.

My heart felt it might burst with pride and I beamed my appreciation. How I had changed! Had I thought in the beginning that I would spend fifteen years filling tea glasses, I would never have come and yet, as he spoke, I knew he had paid me the most enormous compliment. Yes, were it to be written on my tombstone, it would be enough! To know that the Turkish church had felt esteemed and welcome in our home somehow felt like a big 'well done' from God. Ozjan's words seemed to me like another sighting of a hoopoe.

We said farewell to Beshiktash football club. Samim was able to have his photograph taken with national striker Ertugrul and decided that he would work hard in Scotland to develop his ball skills that he might return one day as a player/manager! Emma had a weekend away with the school and some special goodbyes there. Then there was Melis, her friend next door with whom there was an ongoing exchange of gifts, cards and promises of undying love!

Julyan drove our faithful eighteen-year-old Ford Granada to northern Iraq for a final visit, and left her there for the team to use. Despite her age, her body and engine were still strong and we hoped she'd be able to continue her service. He travelled with Andrew, a co-worker and friend of many years, who would be taking on much of Julyan's responsibilities when we left.

A new American family agreed to move into our house and were happy to adopt Katie the cat. We had hoped for a change in the British quarantine laws right up until the end but we had to admit that the arrival of the Morrises was an answer to prayer.

On our last Sunday at church, there were several baptisms. One was a close friend called Jan. The International Fellowship met in its own rented accommodation and for this occasion, we had filled up a bathtub in the basement. There were a few tense moments as Julyan, with eyes and hand raised heavenwards, prayed a longish prayer as his other hand held Jan under the water. It was only later that we understood. Jan had insisted that Julyan hold him under for five full seconds.

It was good to have a girl at the meeting who had visited the bookstall that morning and asked where she could find a church. The baptisms had moved her to tears as she had experienced God's love and witnessed such a visual enactment of the gospel message.

Each Sunday it was now possible to erect a book table free of charge in a busy market area of Istanbul. Christian books, New Testaments and Jesus films could be sold, profitable conversations could take place and enquirers could sign up for the correspondence course. It seemed incredible to find such openness amidst rising Islamic fundamentalism but the situation was complex.

We grieved for Turkey as she opened herself more and more to the West and consequently to permissive Western ways. Pornography and materialism were coming in like a flood and eroding traditional values. Yet, with this new openness to the West came more freedom for Christians and many more opportunities to share the Gospel. We were delighted to donate our folding kitchen table to the bookstall ministry!

Understandably, many Turks were returning to their Islamic roots in an attempt to stem the Western tide, hence the rise in fundamentalism.

Moderate Muslim Turks, however, could often see the hypocrisy of hard-line Islam and began to seek God elsewhere.

We visited Kamil and Hajer for a final tea together. The house was full of relatives but we were able to present them with a nice hard-backed New Testament and a little Bible study on white clothing! As we were about to leave, this righteous man stood up and insisted we accept a rent rebate as we had provided new tenants for him before our month was ended. We tried to refuse but for him it was a matter of honour.

They were very happy with the new American family and perhaps, at a simple level, they were the new white shirt that we had given them. Nevertheless, I determined to keep in touch with them from Scotland and even send Kamil a present of an 'easy-care' white shirt that wouldn't require much ironing for Hajer and would be comfortable and gentle for an ageing neck. I hoped it would fit!

Among our last visitors to say goodbye were our best friends Hasan and Ayshe. We spent our few days together looking back over the years, grateful to God for all he had done in our lives. They would be moving shortly, themselves, to a small provincial town because of Hasan's work. Spiritually, it would be a desert there but remembering God's faithfulness we could all look forward to the future, confident of God's good purposes. Ayshe and Hasan were gifted in language, Turkish and English and Ayshe was developing her communication gift through writing and poetry. As they were about to leave she presented us with a farewell gift. It was a poem she had written and framed entitled, 'Thanks from a Hoopoe'!

> Your warmth gave the welcome
> Your love laid the table
> Your wisdom did the listening
> Your tears poured out the comfort
> Your enthusiasm such an encouragement
> Who for?
> Me!
>
> You shared your very selves
> Opened the depths of your hearts
> And so my heart too was widened
> Who am I?
> The Turkish Hoopoe!

As I read the words there was no sense of pride welling up inside me but rather a deep dawning that God's grace had done all this for me and that these words were really my poem to the Lord.

We packed the van for the long drive to Scotland singing, 'We all live in a yellow transit van' in order to keep our spirits light. Everyone knew what they wanted to take although there was some debate about Julyan's enormous library of books! For me there weren't any special belongings except some soft furnishings and, of course, my Turkish tea glasses and coffee cups.

Then I decided to take our dining table. It had been so central throughout our years in Turkey serving friends from many different countries, some of whom we would never see again this side of Heaven. With its sectioned top and detachable legs, it was possible to make room in the van. What a great reminder of our many precious relationships.

It had known endless pot-lucks and celebrations. As an art table it had seen much cutting and sticking. Visual aids were often made on it for Sunday School and day school. It actually became school for a week when the normal room was flooded because of a burst pipe. It was also great for table tennis, and had taken part in many dramas, once playing the tomb in an Easter production.

It carried many memories but perhaps most of all it reminded me that God can spread a table in the wilderness. He had given me so many good things, so many spiritual hoopoes, people and places, experiences and insights that I wouldn't have missed for the world. I had gone to give yet had received a hundred fold.

Perhaps that was the message I would bring back to Scotland, to a country and a church that had given to the world so much in the past.

Now, consumed by her own weakness and sense of spiritual bankruptcy she felt she had nothing left to offer.

It would be a message of faith and hope that the God of miracles who fed a multitude with a little lunch pack, offered through the hands of the apostle Andrew, our Patron Saint, would again put his arm around our shoulders and make us brave to give again and take our rightful place in the worldwide missionary force. The task of going to the unreached abroad or the lost at home would not be done without us. I wanted to shout to Scotland as loud as I could that in giving and in going:

'You Will See Hoopoes!'

DISTINCTIVES

Vaughan Roberts

ISBN 1–85078–331–4

In a fresh and readable style, the author of *Turning Points*, Vaughan Roberts issues a challenging call to Christians to live out their faith. We should be different from the world around us — Christian distinctives should set us apart in how we live, think, act and speak. Targeting difficult and crucial areas such as our attitude to money and possessions, sexuality, contentment, relativism and service, this is holiness in the tradition of J.C. Ryle for the contemporary generation.

- Will you take up the challenge?
- Will you dare to be different?

Vaughan Roberts is rector of St Ebbe's Church, Oxford. He is a popular conference speaker and University Christian Union speaker.

OM
publishing

OUT OF THE COMFORT ZONE

George Verwer

ISBN 1–85077–353–5

Reading this book could seriously change your attitude! George Verwer has managed to write a book that is humble and hard-hitting at the same time. He doesn't pull any punches in his heart's cry for a 'grace-awakened' approach to mission, and wants to cut through superficial 'spirituality' that may be lurking inside you. George Verwer is known throughout the world as a motivator and mobiliser. *Out of the Comfort Zone* should only be read by those who are willing to accept God's grace, catch His vision and respond with action in the world of mission.

OM
publishing

OPERATION WORLD

PRAY FOR THE WORLD

Patrick Johnstone

ISBN 1-85078-120-6

The definitive guide to praying effectively and specifically for every country of the world, formatted for daily use, or to dip into when praying for missionaries or around current events. Using this book is an excellent way to involve yourself in global mission.

STOP, CHECK, GO

Ditch Townsend

ISBN 1-85078-364-0

Anyone planning on going overseas on a short-term missions trip should soak up the contents of this invaluable book. Helping them to prepare practically, personally and spiritually, this superb book will ensure that the benefits of the experience are greatly increased to all concerned.

OM
publishing